AMERICAN AUTHORS AND CRITICS SERIES

GENERAL EDITOR

JOHN MAHONEY

University of Detroit

EMILY DICKINSON ABOUT 1848

Photographed from an original daguerreotype; the only authentic portrait of Emily Dickinson later than childhood.

EMILY

DICKINSON

An Introduction and Interpretation

JOHN B. PICKARD

University of Florida

HOLT, RINEHART AND WINSTON, INC.

New York · Chicago · San Francisco · Toronto · London

Barnes & Noble, Inc., is the exclusive distributor of the hard-bound edition of this title.

Appreciation is expressed to Dick Epler of Barnes and Noble for his critical assistance and constant encouragement and to Mrs. Patricia Harris Burgin, formerly of Barnes and Noble, for her original suggestions and confidence that I should do this book.

Letters and poems herein quoted are reprinted by permission of the publishers. Poem numbers* 216, 88, 441, 214, 67, 389, 712, 228, 1332, 1405, 1493, 328, 1356, 986, 1575, 812, 1540, 130, 290, 1068, 585, 401, 303, 530, 528, 561, 510, 341, 465, 280, 287, 1393, 1581, 501, 1159, 1454, 883 are reprinted by permission of the publishers and the Trustees of Amherst College from Thomas H. Johnson, Editor, *The Poems of Emily Dickinson,* Cambridge, Mass.: The Belknap Press of Harvard University Press, Copyright 1951, 1955, by The President and Fellows of Harvard College.

Numbers 822, 1135, 1295, 1670 Copyright 1914, 1942 by Martha Dickinson Bianchi; numbers 293, 370, 406, 515, 721, 745, 754, 827, 1196 Copyright 1929, © 1957 by Mary L. Hampson; numbers 286, 369 Copyright 1935, © 1963 by Martha Dickinson Bianchi from *The Complete Poems of Emily Dickinson* edited by Thomas H. Johnson, by permission of Little, Brown and Co., and The Belknap Press of Harvard University Press.

* The numbers listed are those assigned to the poems and letters in the Johnson editions of Emily Dickinson's works. The poems are listed by title with their Johnson numbers in the Index.

Poem numbers 1072 and 1545, from *The Life and Letters of Emily Dickinson*, edited by Martha D. Bianchi; number 1454, from *Emily Dickinson Face to Face*, edited by Martha Dickinson Bianchi are reprinted by permission of Houghton Mifflin Company and The Belknap Press of Harvard University Press.

Letters numbered 260, 261, 268, 271, 342a, 243b, 108, 86, 1, 8, 15, 39, 18, 153, 29, 110, 77, 157, 233, 801, 776, 489, 249, 277, 298, 204, 932, 950, 388, 450, 285, 286, 444a, 937a, 559, 868, 459a, 332, 108, 193, 503, 184, 319, 750 are reprinted by permission of the publishers from Thomas H. Johnson and Theodora V. W. Ward, editors, *The Letters of Emily Dickinson*, Cambridge, Mass.: The Belknap Press of Harvard University Press, Copyright 1958, The President and Fellows of Harvard College.

Acknowledgment is also made to Yale University Press for permission to quote from *The Years and Hours of Emily Dickinson* by Jay Leyda, Copyright © 1960 by Yale University Press

All works quoted are listed in the Selected Bibliography following the text.

ABOUT THE AUTHOR

JOHN B. PICKARD teaches at the University of Florida. In addition to numerous articles published in *College English, The New England Quarterly, American Literature* and other professional journals, his writing and editing includes *John Greenleaf Whittier* (another title in the American Authors and Critics Series) and *Legends of New England* by John Greenleaf Whittier. He is currently editing the collected letters of Whittier.

PREFACE

Emily Dickinson is part of a stark tradition—one that includes philosophers and poets from Edward Taylor to Robert Frost. Her intense preoccupation with pain, death, and immortality typified the introspective Puritan conscience, while her terse poetic shorthand reflected New England traits of frugality and conciseness. Like Thoreau, Dickinson searched within the recesses of her spirit, and her poetry reveals the soul's infinite capacity for awareness.

The mysteriousness of Emily Dickinson's personality baffled friends and outsiders, while her unique poetic method led later editors to conventionalize and alter her poems. The tangle of legends and myths associated with her family relationships, love attachments, and eventual seclusion coupled with the fragmentary editing of her poetry prevented a true measure of her genius until the 1950s. Only with Charles Anderson's book in 1960 was there a full critical examination of her creative process and poetic significance. The present book attempts a further exploration of her unusual personality and, by combining biography with extensive analyses of her outstanding poems, intends to measure the extent of her poetic achievement.

This book was written for college students in a special sense, for it grew directly from my own classroom teaching of Emily Dickinson's poetry at Rice University. Scores of students in various classes enhanced my understanding and appreciation of her poetry with their comments, questions, discussions, and analyses. This, then, is their book as well as mine.

Gainesville, Florida   J. B. P.
August, 1966.

CONTENTS

	Preface	ix
	Chronology	xiii
	Introduction	1
1	Early Years	7
2	Maturity	18
3	A Poet's Mind	30
4	A Poet's Practice	46
5	Nature	56
6	Social Scene and Love	76
7	Pain and Death	94
8	Immortality	111
9	Achievement	122
	Bibliography	127
	Index	131

ILLUSTRATIONS

Emily Dickinson about 1848	frontispiece
Facsimile of "Safe in their Alabaster Chambers"	44

CHRONOLOGY

1830   Emily Dickinson born December 10, in Amherst, Massachusetts, the second child of Edward and Emily Dickinson. [The Dickinson family had been in New England since the seventeenth century.]

1840   Moved from homestead on Main Street to a new residence. Portrait painted.

1840—1847   Attended Amherst Academy.

1846   Deeply affected by a winter religious revival, but failed to convert.

1847—1848   Attended Mount Holyoke Female Seminary at South Hadley, Massachusetts. Underwent a severe religious crisis in January, but again remained unconverted. Only known photograph taken.

1848—1849   Came under the influence of Ben Newton who widened her reading interests and encouraged her poetic ambitions.

1852   Her first poem, a mock valentine, published in the *Springfield Republican*, February 20. Father elected to Congress.

1855   Spent January and February in Washington, and March in Philadelphia. Presumably heard Reverend Charles Wadsworth preach in Philadelphia. Family moved back to old house on Main Street.

1856   Brother Austin married Sue Gilbert, a close friend.

1858   Began the most creative period of her life. Wrote more than fifty poems during the year and assembled them in fair copies. Drafted first "Master" letter, relating to someone she loved. Formed friendship with Samuel Bowles, editor of the *Springfield Republican*.

1860   Visited by Reverend Charles Wadsworth early in the year.

1861   "The May-Wine" ("I taste a liquor never brewed") published in the *Springfield Republican* on May 4. Drafted two other "Master" letters.

1862   Underwent a great emotional crisis during the winter, possibly associated with Charles Wadsworth's departure for California or Samuel Bowles' trip to Europe. "The Sleeping" ("Safe in their Alabaster Chambers") published in the *Springfield Republican* on March 1. Wrote 366 poems during the year. Initiated correspondence with Thomas W. Higginson on April 15, seeking literary advice. By June, determined to remain a private poet, she gradually withdrew from society.

1863—1865   Wrote nearly 400 poems.

1864   "My Sabbath" ("Some keep the Sabbath going to Church") published in *The Round Table* on March 12; and "Sunset" ("Blazing in Gold and quenching in Purple") published in the *Springfield Republican* on March 30. Went to Boston for eye treatments.

1866   "The Snake" ("A narrow Fellow in the Grass") published in the *Springfield Republican* on February 14. Ended her main creative period, after composing over 1000 poems in eight years.

1870   Visited by Thomas W. Higginson on August 16. Her poetic interests were renewed in the early 1870s and she wrote nearly 200 poems.

1873   Second and last visit of Thomas W. Higginson on December 3. Began friendship with Helen Hunt Jackson.

1874   Father died on June 16. Turned to an old family friend, Judge Otis Lord, for consolation. Entered into complete seclusion.

1877—1884   Friendship with Judge Otis Lord developed into a love attachment after the death of Lord's wife. Considered marriage, but the care of her invalid mother [since 1875] and his ill-health prevented it.

1878   Samuel Bowles died. At the suggestion of Helen Hunt Jackson "Success" ("Success is counted sweetest") published in an anonymous volume, *A Masque of Poets*.

1880   Visited by Charles Wadsworth for the last time, during the summer.

1882   Charles Wadsworth died in April, and her mother in November.

1883   The death of her favorite nephew, Gilbert, deeply affected her.

1884 After the death of Judge Otis Lord in March, suffered a nervous collapse.

1885 Ill during the fall and confined to bed.

1886 Died on May 15 at the age of fifty-five. Her sister Lavinia burned most of her correspondence but saved the poems.

1890 First edition of her poetry published, edited by Mabel Loomis Todd [a neighbor] and Thomas W. Higginson. For the next sixty years relatives and friends published selections from her poems.

1955 Complete edition of her poems published in three volumes by Thomas H. Johnson.

INTRODUCTION

O N AN April Wednesday in 1862 Thomas Wentworth Higginson reluctantly took some letters from the Worcester post office. He probably suspected that they contained still more demands for literary advice, occasioned by his recent article in the *Atlantic Monthly*. In the lead story for the April issue, "Letter to a Young Contributor," he gave practical advice to aspiring writers. Mainly counseling against rhetorical phrasing and redundancy, he urged: "Charge your style with life. . . . there may be years of crowded passion in a word, a half a life in a sentence. Such being the majesty of the art you seek to practise, you can at least take time and deliberation before dishonoring it."

One letter he received was written in a hesitant, individual manner, as if the writer's style had been formed by studying "fossil birdtracks." It was unsigned, but the writer's name, Emily Dickinson, was written on a card and enclosed in an envelope. The contents of the letter were even stranger:

> Are you too deeply occupied to say if my Verse is alive?
> The Mind is so near itself—it cannot see, distinctly—and I have none to ask—
> Should you think it breathed—and had you the leisure to tell me, I should feel quick gratitude—
> If I make the mistake—that you dared to tell me—would give me sincerer honor—toward you—
> I enclose my name—asking you, if you please—Sir—to tell me what is true?
> That you will not betray me—it is needless to ask—since Honor is it's own pawn—[1]

Also enclosed were four poems as samples of her recent work. In a diffident yet cryptic manner she asks not if her verses were good or

---

[1] Throughout this book quotations from the letters and poems of Emily Dickinson will be reprinted without any correction of misspellings, punctuation mistakes, or grammatical errors. For example, in the above quotation Dickinson's incorrect use of "it's" for "its" is retained.

publishable, but if they "breathe" and have vitality. Admitting the artist's inability to judge, she begs him as a literary critic to tell her the truth about the merit of the poems. Her final appeal cleverly echoes his own remarks on honor.

If Higginson was struck by her unique phrasing of an accustomed request, he must have been more puzzled by the poems. Nothing in his literary background could have prepared him to understand their originality or appreciate their artistic perfection. Even though his professional writing was varied and had earned him acceptance within Boston's distinguished cultural circle, it was imitative and quite conventional. Certainly his quick responsiveness to popular taste epitomized the genteel tradition's demand for decent literary subjects, written in a standardized style, and its feeling that good poetry needed regular meters and exact rhymes. Ironically, Higginson had already helped many young writers to publish, but when confronted with an authentic poetic talent he faltered.

One can imagine his confusion as he scanned the opening lines of this poem:

> Safe in their Alabaster Chambers—
> Untouched by Morning
> And untouched by Noon—
> Lie the meek members of the Resurrection—
> Rafter of Satin—and Roof of Stone!

In these lines alone he must have noted the inexact rhyme of "Noon" and "Stone," the irregular iambic pentameter (missing or added feet), the strange use of dashes, and the erratic capitalization. How could his mind, attuned to the bland platitudes of Longfellow's "A Psalm of Life," have caught the subtle satire of religious orthodoxy and the delicate interplay of imagery and sound in "Alabaster," "Chambers," "Satin," and "Stone"?

Though he remarked after receiving poems from Emily Dickinson and other young poets, "I forsee that 'Young Contributors' will send me worse things than ever now," he was intrigued by her work and promptly answered her letter. Avoiding her central question about the verse's merit, he asked her age, how long she had been writing, what she enjoyed reading, and finally advised her to read Walt Whitman (whom he did not like). Her answers must have been most perplexing to a man of Higginson's temperament, a man who met strangers openly and found writing natural and easy. Enclosing more poems, she commented: "I sing, as the Boy does by the Burying Ground—because I am afraid—" and then went on to talk mysteriously about two former tutors who had left her. Of her family she wrote: "My Mother does not care for thought—and Father, too busy with his Briefs—to notice what we do—He buys me many Books— but begs me not to read them—because he fears they joggle the Mind." Obviously she dramatized these personal remarks to gain Higginson's attention and keep his interest. So she naïvely stated that she had "made no verse—but one or two—until this winter— Sir," when she had already composed at least three hundred poems over a five-year span and was sending him only the ones she considered most successful. Even then she clearly established her independence by dismissing his advice on reading Whitman, because she had been told that *Leaves of Grass* was disgraceful.

However, her replies gave Higginson sorely needed insights into her mind and interests, and he responded by praising the beauty and force of her verses. Still, he criticized her style as "spasmodic" and "uncontrolled" and advised that she delay publishing until she had mastered form. Her answer to this letter on June 7, 1862, was a crucial one and set the tone for their future correspondence. Having learned from someone she believed qualified to judge that her verses were unpublishable, she accepted this opinion as an unalterable fact. Characteristically she thanked him for his justice in criticizing her imperfect rhymes, but added that she could not "drop the Bells whose jingling cooled my Tramp." Fully aware of her unusual rhyming, she utilized their "jingling" for effects Higginson could never appreciate. Yet on the central issue she agreed: "I smile when you suggest that I delay 'to publish'—that being foreign to my thought, as Firmament to Fin. . . . My Barefoot-Rank is better." So the decision to remain a private poet was irrevocably made. However painful Higginson's initial "surgery" or however exhilarating his later "Domingo" praise, she now cast him in a new role. He was to become her "Preceptor," a sympathetic correspondent who would discuss books with her, keep her in contact with the literary world, and read her verses. She signed this letter "Your friend" and the next one as his scholar. Thus she established the open pretense that he would teach her how to write acceptable verses, though she would never follow his advice. And he knew it.

The succeeding letters continued to be elusive, affording only enigmatic views of her personal and artistic life. She told him that her business was "Circumference" and that she could not organize or control her poetic power. Coyly she blamed her own ignorance on her failure to correct her poetic deviations and adroitly fenced his query about her avoidance of men and women by answering: "They talk of Hallowed things, aloud—and embarrass my Dog." Then with an arch juxtaposition, perhaps satirizing Higginson's inept attempts at criticism, she observed: "I think Carl [her dog] would please you —He is dumb, and brave." Thoroughly bewildered and even doubtful of her sanity, he recognized her pathetic, almost neurotic, need for sympathy and became her tutor. It is to his credit that for nearly twenty-five years he continued to encourage her writing and offer consolation for her trying personal problems. Perhaps he never knew how much this relationship meant to her. Later she wrote that he preserved her life—and she meant just that, for he became the sympathetic, detached listener to whom she could reveal her poetic insights and personal tensions. In a sense these letters provided the therapy that healed the emotional wounds received from her searing love experience in the 1860s.

Thus occurred one of the memorable events in American literary history as Emily Dickinson decided to remain unknown and unpublished. Why she chose Higginson as her mentor and accepted his judgment as final cannot be fully comprehended until the social and cultural background of her life and the emotional crisis of the 1860s are examined. Perhaps she admired Higginson's frequent *Atlantic Monthly* contributions; perhaps his article on publishing came when she most needed outside literary advice. Still, one could wish that, like Whitman, she had sent her poetry to Ralph Waldo Emerson. It is interesting to ponder what might have happened had she received from Emerson the praise he gave an unknown Whitman: "I am not blind to the worth of this wonderful gift of *Leaves of Grass*. I find it the most extraordinary piece of wit and wisdom that America has yet contributed. . . . I greet you at the beginning of a great career." Such praise was not forthcoming, and perhaps it was best. A reading public that ignored *Moby Dick* and condemned Whitman's poetry as immoral certainly could not respond to her individual style and unorthodox analysis of human emotions.

What Higginson truly felt about his strange correspondent can only be conjectured. Certainly her sudden flashes of wit baffled him, while her startling personal remarks and critical aloofness both annoyed and fascinated him. Often struck by the beauty and vigor of her poetry, he still questioned its literary value. The "person" interested him far more than the "poet." He asked for her photograph, puzzled over her ability to endure such isolation, invited her to Boston, and after eight years finally went to Amherst to meet her. His record of this meeting remains the most revealing personal account we have of her conversation and appearance. His main response was a consciousness of extreme tension and decided strength. "I never was with anyone who drained my nerve power so much. Without touching her, she drew from me. I am glad not to live near her." Like a consummate actress she had carefully planned her entrance. A copy of one of Higginson's books was on the table and he was made to wait alone until

> in glided a little plain woman with two smooth bands of reddish hair . . . with no good feature—in a very plain and exquisitely clean white pique & blue net worsted shawl. She came to me with two day lilies which she put in a sort of childlike way into my hand & said, 'These are my introduction' in a soft frightened breathless childlike voice—& added under her breath Forgive me if I am frightened; I never see strangers & hardly know what I say.

Startled, he watched her as a playgoer at a performance, listening while she talked continuously and brilliantly. Though he patronizingly called her his eccentric poetess and wondered why the insane clung to him, her personality and epigrammatic conversation so impressed him that he recorded her aphorisms:

> Women talk: men are silent: that is why I dread women. How do most people live without any thoughts. There are many people in the world (you must have noticed them in the street) How do they live. How do they get strength to put on their clothes in the morning. I find ecstasy in living—the mere sense of living is joy enough.

If she was a riddle that Higginson never solved, she was equally a paradox to her family and friends. For neighbors and later generations she became a fascinating legend, probably as "dear, inescapable, impervious, tranquil and perverse" to Amherst inhabitants as Emily Grierson was to her townspeople in Faulkner's "A Rose for Emily." To outsiders her life seemed a series of mannerisms and perplexing withdrawals: she always dressed in white, never left her father's house, refused to see close friends, often received visitors while hidden behind a slightly opened door, theatrically lowered baskets of cookies to children from her upstairs room, and sometimes sent notes concealed in the stems of flowers. As the years lengthened, the stories about her seclusion assumed romantic proportions. Her father was supposed to have severed an early love affair by dramatically driving the young man from the house; she was said to have been in love with a married man whom she renounced after a climactic meeting; and, too, she was considered immoral, having been seen in the arms of a trusted family friend. To separate facts from the mass of rumor and speculation has been the task of a generation. Only by fully investigating her New England background and family relations can one hope to uncover the approximate truth about her romantic attachments, her turn to poetry, and her seclusion. It is at once a tribute to her personality and a source of constant frustration for her biographers that she veiled her inner life so successfully for so long.

1

EARLY YEARS

THE AMHERST into which Emily Dickinson was born on December 10, 1830, was a small New England farm community of less than three thousand people. Located in the center of a huge amphitheater of hills, it was considered a beauty spot in the rich farmlands of the Connecticut River valley. Over a hundred miles west of Boston, Amherst had thus far resisted the liberal Unitarian movement and the more advanced social influences of the larger mercantile centers. In fact, Amherst College had been proudly founded nine years before to "check the progress of errors which are propagated from Cambridge." As a self-contained remnant of orthodox Calvinism, the town was slowly becoming an anachronism within its own valley area. Certainly its cultural and religious roots extended far back into the region's past and seemed solidly planted. This entire section had formerly been the stronghold of Solomon Stoddard, a Northampton minister. He ruled the whole Hampshire district for over fifty years, 1672-1729, with such autocratic power and defiance of the Boston ministry that he was called "Pope" Stoddard. His loosening of the restrictions placed upon church membership greatly increased his congregation and gave him a popular following that backed his liberal tendencies. However, his successor, Jonathan Edwards, was disturbed by the increasing emotionalism and temporary nature of the conversions fostered by the periodic revivals that swept rural New England. He doubted the sincerity of these conversions and tried to bring his Northampton congregation back to the basic strengths of Calvinism: that man is depraved and conceived in original sin and that salvation (election) is unconditionally given by God to a select few. But even the brilliant and forceful Jonathan Edwards could not restrain mercantile demands for the separation of business and religion or the popular desire for an individualistic, humanitarian religion. Eventually, in 1755, Edwards' Northampton parish dismissed him. The forces that defeated him also spawned the Unitarian movement of the next century, which was in turn replaced by Emerson's more liberal Transcendentalism.

Yet the Calvinistic religious consciousness never completely lost vitality in the valley towns like Amherst. The churches in the town were orthodox Congregational ones, and services were held twice on Sunday—with daily Bible reading in most homes. Sermons stressed doom and God's vengeance and these mournful ideas were re-echoed in hymns like "That awful day will surely come" and "Broad is the road that leads to death." In particular, this area still witnessed the familiar revival harvest of lost souls, and constant demands were made upon church members to declare themselves for Christ. So Emily Dickinson was born into a community where evangelical devoutness permeated every action. Though she was repelled by Calvinism's grim dogmas and spent her life rebelling against them, she never escaped its eschatological emphasis. She was continually preoccupied with death, resurrection, immortality, and judgment and never ceased examining the undeniable reality of God. Her almost obsessive concern with death (she wrote more than five hundred lyrics on the subject), fascination with pain, and contemplation of religious experience reveal her attachment to basic Calvinism. In fact, as Allen Tate has brilliantly argued in his article "New England Culture and Emily Dickinson," she was born into a perfect literary situation. Since the older religious beliefs seemed invalidated and the community failed to supply sufficient moral or cultural supports, she was forced to examine critically these traditions in the light of her own experience and to discover anew their enduring values. Tate calls Emily Dickinson's task one of defining culture, that is, rediscovering the source of ideas and standards which had become obscured by dogma and practicality. However it might be phrased, the tensions resulting from the clash of her perceptive, inquiring mind with the rigidly orthodox community produced some of her finest poems.

Though the Calvinist influence upon her life was fundamental, her New England heritage was of equal importance. Like most Amherst inhabitants, she saw the world in a New England fashion and lived according to its century-tested practices of industry, moderation, duty, and thrift. She found little humor and even less poetry in this existence, for at its core was an acute moral sensitivity, austere self-discipline, and intense awareness of one's public responsibility. The Bible was the great law and the religious center of this world, while the home and family were equally revered. "Save or starve" was not just a copybook maxim to be memorized and forgotten; and, at the height of her poetic power, Emily Dickinson was frugally writing her poems on bits of scrap paper, on the backs of old envelopes, and on discarded bills. Her father had horses and barnyard animals and raised his own vegetables. The women cooked and cleaned with water carried from wells, made their own clothing, and struggled to keep warm through the long winters; theirs was a hardy, exhausting existence, with the "prickly art" of housekeeping consuming most of their time. Relaxation was limited to simple social visits and family exchanges. Cards, dancing, and novel reading were still prohibited in 1830, and formal dinners were considered too sophisticated. The major social events in Amherst were the College commencement in late summer and the fall Cattle Show, both being held with special ceremonies and extensive exhibitions. The town's insular complacency and habitual fondness for gossip could be stifling and even cruel, and the wife of one of Amherst's many dismissed ministers was expressing a common complaint when she wrote that her husband had been barbarously treated and that "even the New Zelanders [sic] would have behaved better."

This was Amherst, with its limitations and strengths reflected in Emily Dickinson's poetry. As George Whicher has succinctly phrased it in *This Was a Poet*: "To an extraordinary degree she absorbed into herself the atmosphere of the countryside where she was born. . . . She made it her business to embody in her poems the quintessence of New England ways of thinking and feeling. In her the region became articulate."

The house into which Emily Dickinson was born, lived most of her life, and died was one of the few solid red-brick mansions in Amherst. Built by her grandfather to serve as a successful country lawyer's residence, it stood as a tangible symbol of the Dickinson achievement—the heritage of six generations in America. Though he was an outstanding Amherst lawyer, Samuel Fowler Dickinson wanted to be a minister and so with missionary zeal spent his life and money fostering Christian education. In 1814 he originated the movement to found Amherst Academy and almost singlehandedly organized the college a few years later. He so completely devoted his time and finances to the school that by 1830 he was impoverished. When he was forced to sell his homestead he sought a new life in the Middle West, where he died in 1838, characteristically serving another church college, Western Reserve. His eldest son, Edward Dickinson, balanced his father's intense concern for Christian education with a realistic secular interest in his own prosperity. Though devoted to Amherst College which he faithfully assisted as treasurer for nearly forty years, concerned for his town which he served numerous times as a state legislator, and loyal to his Hampshire district which he once represented as a United States Congressman, he made certain that his law practice thrived and repaired the family honor by repurchasing the homestead in 1855. Even more than his father, Edward Dickinson embodied all the aristocratic qualities of a small-town squire. A letter to his future wife typifies his life's concern that "we be virtuous, intelligent, industrious and by the exercise of every virtue, & the cultivation of every excellence, be esteemed & respected & beloved by all—We must determine to do our duty to each other."

Throughout his life he was guided by this stern sense of duty. Righteous and rigid, he never allowed his emotions to interfere with his role as a responsible leader of the town. Even his religious conversion, which waited until he was forty-seven, was later phrased in a dry legal manner and officially dated: "I hereby give myself to God. Edward Dickinson. May 1, 1873." He ruled his house like an absolute monarch, rearing his children with full assurance that they would become Christian citizens. At his death his son Austin is supposed to have kissed him, remarking, "There, Father, I never dared to do that while you were living." Emily's comments on her father, scattered throughout her correspondence, are justly famous, though they usually hide her genuine love and respect behind a satiric pose. Family relations were never easy for Edward Dickinson. He was devoted to Austin and missed the boy dreadfully while he was studying at Harvard; yet, according to Emily, they did nothing but "fisticuff" while together.

Although Emily laughed at his pompousness and chafed under his filial demands, she knew his other sides: the father who loved fast horses, who rang the town bells to make the villagers witness a display of northern lights, who went to the barn in his slippers across the snow to feed hungry birds. Emily could remember the open enjoyment he had in her company the last Sunday afternoon before his death. As their visit ended he remarked in a rare display of affection, almost embarrassing his daughter, that he wished the afternoon would never end. While he lived he remained the focal point of his children's lives and molded the family into a closely knit patriarchal group.

His death in 1874 put the final seal on Emily's seclusion. She later wrote to Higginson that her father's spirit was so pure and awesome that she could not imagine any other like it in existence. Throughout the remainder of her life she never stopped recording the terrible sense of anguish that his death occasioned. She owed him much of what Millicent Todd Bingham called "the Dickinson Difference," and when she wondered what made the Dickinsons different from others she may have had in mind her father's moral firmness, community responsibility, and intense self-awareness. Of her mother she remarked, "I never had a mother. I suppose a mother is one to whom you hurry when you are troubled." Certainly her mother remained a submissive, shadowy figure in the family group, one who is characterized by her own remark in a family letter: "I think of nothing interesting to say." A year after her husband's death she became paralyzed. Emily assumed complete care for the bedridden invalid and spent the next seven years devotedly nursing her. It was only during these years, with the mother-child roles reversed, that Emily realized a love for her mother.

Her older brother Austin understood Emily better than any other member of her family. He was particularly close to her while he studied at Harvard and during the courtship of his future wife, Sue Gilbert. Although he possessed humor and aesthetic appreciation, he lacked his father's dominant personality and moral certainty. Edward Dickinson checked Austin's early desire to go West by building him a stylish mansion next door to the family home and by taking him in as a law partner. The family bonds were securely tightened when Austin succeeded his father as treasurer of Amherst College. Always a follower, Austin remained a pale imitation of his father, withdrawing more into himself until Emily remarked of his four-week stay with them in 1874 that he never seemed to be emotionally or mentally present. Austin's wife, Sue Gilbert, was Emily's closest friend in the early 1850s and throughout the course of a stormy friendship received nearly three hundred poems from Emily. Sue had an independent mind, a tart wit, and took a frank delight in conversation and lavish dinner parties. Her entertainments were social occasions in Amherst, and one visitor at her commencement tea wrote that she was "a really brilliant and highly cultivated woman of great taste and refinement, perhaps a little too aggressive, a little too sharp in wit and repartee, and a little too ambitious for social prestige, but, withal, a woman of the world in the best sense." Her social and family interests, coupled with a detached, often critical attitude toward Emily's unrestrained affection, gradually alienated Emily. A break came in the 1870s as Emily's earlier affection changed to hurt withdrawal. Regardless of their altered relationship, Sue shared more of Emily's personal life and poetic hopes than any other single contemporary.

Lavinia, Emily's younger sister, completes the family group. Aggressive and practical as Emily was withdrawn and sensitive, Vinnie spent her life protecting her sister's privacy and fulfilling her social obligations. A personality in her own right, with a frank, caustic manner, her bond with Emily was deep and unbreakable. After her sister's death a shocked Vinnie discovered the mass of hidden poems and demanded first of Sue, then of a neighbor, Mabel Loomis Todd, and finally of Colonel Higginson that the poems be published. She had little appreciation for the poems, but felt they had to be the works of a genius and must be given to the world. A pathetic, rigidly determined spinster, she singlehandedly forced the publication of her sister's poems. As the last member of her family she lived long enough to see the poems achieve popular success.

Of Emily's childhood very little is known. She grew up in a secure, well-ordered family, with a father deeply concerned for his children's welfare. Edward Dickinson's letters while away from home showed his affection for the children and were filled with practical advice for their behavior. In one note to Emily he warned her to guard her health, to be pleasant to her brother (obviously one of her failings), and to be "one of the best little girls in town." From her earliest years Emily responded to music, and, when she was only three, she learned how to play the piano. Her principal childhood memories concerned the exhilarating freedom of running barefoot through mud and a delight in discovering new flowers. The church with its two Sunday services and home devotions loomed forebodingly in her young life, as it did for all the children. Austin once recalled how the mournful church hymns accompanied by the heavy tones of a double bass viol appalled his young imagination and haunted him into manhood.

Just before the family moved from the homestead to a house on Pleasant Street, a wandering artist painted a group portrait of the three children, with Austin in the center and Emily and Lavinia on either side. Though awkwardly posed and looking more like a picture of a wax manikin than of a young girl, Emily's portrait shows her deep-set serious eyes; in her hands she holds prophetically a moss rose on the open pages of a book. Their large new house where they were to spend the next fifteen years was close to the center of town and beside a cemetery. Funeral processions usually passed the Dickinson house on the way to the cemetery, and it is small wonder that Emily grew up conscious of death—it was impossible to avoid. Later, watching a close friend of hers nearing death, she was so moved by the strange beauty of the dying girl that friends had to lead her away. The event so weighed upon her impressionable, thirteen-year-old mind that she became sick, and only a prolonged visit to Boston dulled the traumatic experience. At twenty-one she rather morbidly pictures her own death: "The other day I tried to think how I should look with my eyes shut, and a little white gown on, and a snowdrop on my breast; and I fancied I heard the neighbors stealing in so softly to look down in my face—so fast asleep—so still. . . . I think of the grave very often, and how much it has got of mine, and whether I can ever stop it from carrying off what I love."

During the fall of 1840 Emily attended Amherst Academy. Staffed mainly by former Amherst College students, the school offered a wide range of studies, including the newest courses in science. Though ill health kept her from attending consecutive terms, she remained in the Academy for nearly seven years, practicing the piano, receiving instruction in German, Latin, biology, geology, history, and philosophy. Once she commented to the Harvard-trained Higginson that she had little formal education. Still, she had no need for apology. Before her year at Mount Holyoke she had obtained a far better education than most Americans received from their district school days. A former teacher recollected that, despite her nervousness, she was a bright student, particularly attracting attention and envy for her compositions. In fact, from the beginning her letters demonstrated her individuality and literary ability. Her first extant letter, written when she was twelve, was sent to her brother Austin, who was away at school:

> As Father was going to Northampton and thought of coming over to see you I thought I would improve the opportunity and write you a few lines—We miss you very much indeed you cannot think how odd it seems without you there was always such a Hurrah wherever you was I miss My bedfellow very much for it is rare that I can get any now for Aunt Elisabeth is afraid to sleep alone and Vinnie has to sleep with her but I have the privilege of looking under the bed every night which I improve as you may suppose.

Like a conscientious New England daughter she writes to "improve the opportunity," catches her brother's character by noting his missing loud "Hurrah," and deftly hits at her Aunt Elisabeth's fears of sleeping alone. The letter rushes on with almost no punctuation save a few dashes and is sprinkled with bewildering capitalizations—traits which the mature writer never lost.

During her years at the Academy, Emily was part of an intimate group of five schoolmates, and she corresponded widely with separated friends, especially Abiah Root and Jane Humphrey. Her letters were alternately sentimental and sententious, filled with the usual romantic clichés, tears, treasured locks of hair, and hidden references to beaux. Always she pleaded for more letters, dramatizing her situation and revealing her overaffectionate nature. Sometimes she nostalgically remembered past times with friends or philosophized about separation, but usually she was able to laugh at her sentimentality, calling herself the beauty of Amherst, surrounded by groups of admirers. Through all these early letters one senses her exuberance with life, her delight in picturesque description, and her budding attempts to create a style. In the following letter she is already exploring what was to be the subject matter for great poems like "As imperceptibly as Grief," the change of seasons and the illusory quality of beauty:

> Since I wrote you last, the summer is past and gone, and autumn with the sere and yellow leaf is already upon us. I never knew the time to pass so swiftly, it seems to me, as the past summer. I really think some one must have oiled his chariot wheels, for I don't recollect of hearing him pass, and I am sure I should if something had not prevented his chariot wheels from creaking as usual.

Though overliterary and tritely phrased, the conceit is clever and consciously worked out.

During the winter of 1846 when Amherst witnessed one of its periodic revivals, Abiah Root experienced an ordeal of conversion. As Theodora Ward has remarked: "In the awakening period of adolescence, conversion was looked for by solicitous elders and applauded by contemporaries who had already passed through its throes. To become a practicing Christian was in a sense analogous to the initiation rites of primitive peoples, by which the adolescent becomes a responsible member of the tribe." As her letters reveal, Emily was deeply affected by the need for conversion. Somewhat dramatically, but with sincere distress, she tells Abiah that she has missed the winter meetings because her personality is too excitable and she fears self-deception. She regrets not being a Christian and attempts to analyze why she continues to resist. Moved by Abiah's final conversion and desperately trying to explain her own position, she says that she is unable to resist the lure of the world and has lost her interest in spiritual things. Only fifteen, she is obviously concerned about her unregenerate condition, fearing that she is about to plunge into a terrible abyss. Despite the hackneyed pulpit language, the letters display her suffering and open envy of those who could find peace by submitting to orthodox conversion. But final conversion was repugnant to her questioning, pragmatic mind.

Soul-searching was common for the young—the accepted and normal heritage of Calvinistic training and evangelical fervor. Outwardly Emily lived a normal, secure life, psychologically adjusted to these religious pressures as she was conditioned to the authority of her father. The ordinary social activities filled her life: picnics, walks, sleigh rides, a Poetry of Motion group which sinned by dancing, and even a Shakespeare club where Emily and her girl friends refused to read an expurgated version of the plays. By now her sole ambition was to attend Mount Holyoke Seminary, though she had the maturity to discern that she usually anticipated too much and found her dreams blown away by the actual events. In a similar vein she sentimentally described the beauty and charm of a teacher, adding: "Forgive my glowing description, for you know I am always in love with my teachers." During her last term at the Academy she came under the influence of Leonard Humphrey. A former Amherst College valedictorian with a driving personality and slight invalidism, he was a romantic figure when he became principal of the Academy. Whether he looked upon Emily as anything more than a bright student was improbable, though her letters at this time dwelt often on imaginary love situations. Her comments after his sudden death in 1850 indicated that she idolized him and considered him one of her first "masters," a man who quickened her emotional and mental development: "My master has gone to rest, and the open leaf of the book, and the scholar at school *alone,* make the tears come, and I cannot brush them away; I would not if I could, for they are the only tribute I can pay the departed Humphrey . . . this is my first affliction, and indeed 'tis hard to bear it." At the end of this gloomy, somewhat affected letter is a typical Dickinson shift: "The shore is safer, Abiah, but I love to buffet the sea . . . I love the danger! You are learning control and firmness. Christ Jesus will love you more. I'm afraid he dont love me *any!*"

Poised between childhood and maturity and aware of herself as a personality, she entered Mount Holyoke for the fall term of 1847. The school was situated in South Hadley, only ten miles from Amherst, and had been recently opened by Miss Mary Lyon, a pioneer in women's education. Though primarily concerned with the students' intellectual attainments, Miss Lyon closely supervised their religious activities as well. Many of the teachers were former missionaries, and the graduates often married ministers or devoted their lives to evangelical work. One's spiritual life was hardly a private affair under such conditions and the girls were continually urged to convert. Emily's adjustment to her new life was quick and all-absorbing, as a rigid scholastic routine demanded her full attention. Her typical day was a grueling experience by any college standard. She rose at six, breakfasted at seven, began studying at eight, had devotions at nine, and went to her first class soon afterwards.

> At 10¼. I recite a review of Ancient History, in connection with which we read, Goldsmith & Grimshaw. At. 11. I recite a lesson in 'Pope's Essay on Man' which is merely transposition. At. 12. I practise Calisthenics & at 12¼ read until dinner, which is at 12½ & after dinner, from 1½ until 2 I sing in Seminary Hall. From 2¾ until 3¾. I practise upon the Piano. At 3¾ I go to Sections, where we give in all our accounts for the day, including, Absence—Tardiness—Communications—Breaking Silent Study hours—Receiving Company in our rooms & ten thousand other things which I will not take time or place to mention. At 4½. we go into Seminary Hall, & receive advice from Miss Lyon in the form of a lecture. We have Supper at 6. & silent study hours from then until the retiring bell, which rings at 8¾, but the tardy bell does not ring until 9¾, so that we dont often obey the first warning to retire.

Yet she thrived under these demands and did well in her courses. After a family reunion during the Thanksgiving break, she returned for her winter term to take courses in chemistry, algebra, logic, and physiology and to encounter a major religious crisis. During the fall, regular classes had begun for the unconverted and by December signs of a revival were evident at the school. Miss Lyon personally conferred with the unrepentant, while sermons and lectures stressed the doom of "Sinners in the Hands of an Angry God." Emily's written comments show how distressed she was by the religious pressures. With sixteen others she voluntarily attended special meetings for those who felt "unusually anxious to choose the service of God." However near she came to conversion, the feeling passed and by May, after an illness at home, she wrote that she doubted if such a moment was to be hers again. It never was.

Why she again veered away from professing an orthodox belief can only be conjectured. Although intensely concerned with the salvation of her soul and deeply aware of spiritual reality, she must have ultimately felt a public demonstration of faith incompatible with her more profound religious needs. Struggling against great social and intellectual pressures, she made her first major withdrawal in order to preserve individuality and to experience life on her own unique terms. With the close of the summer term, Emily completed her formal education and was now ready to enter the tumultuous years of the 1850s, which brought full emotional maturity and final poetic development.

The only known photograph of Emily also dates from the Mount Holyoke period. The dominant impression is that of an unformed, sensitive girl whose large eyes unflinchingly challenge the viewer. These expressive brown eyes and thick auburn hair drawn back tightly were the only good features in an otherwise plain freckled face. She called herself the "only Kangaroo among the Beauty" and noted that she was "small, like the Wren, and my Hair is bold, like the Chestnut Bur—and my eyes, like the Sherry in the Glass, that the Guest leaves." Even at this time she was noted for her imaginative phrasing and epigrammatic wit, which flashed only within the family group or with close friends.

From these first eighteen years one catches tantalizing glimpses of the uneven growth of an inquiring intellect and poetic imagination. Her letters disclose a sensitive, overemotional nature which exaggerated slights and timidly withdrew when her affections were not reciprocated. Her amateur philosophizing and sentimental style were typical of her age, as was her concern with death. If she magnified small incidents and dwelt on trivia, she also knew how to draw humor and satire out of the most unlikely material. The wit in her early letters attests to a developing sense of style and feeling for realistic detail. Most important, her spiritual courage and integrity had been tested by two severe religious experiences out of which she had somehow preserved her uncommitted position. Never again was she to experience such religious anguish, but it had toughened her delicate spirit for the harder emotional crises that lay ahead. Childhood and education were ended, but how the woman was to develop remained uncertain as Emily returned to Amherst in August of 1848.

2

MATURITY

O NE OF Emily Dickinson's early letters to Higginson answered a question about her previous life by cryptically remarking: "When a little Girl, I had a friend, who taught me Immortality—but venturing too near, himself—he never returned—Soon after, my Tutor, died—and for several years, my Lexicon—was my only companion—Then I found one more—but he was not contented I be his scholar—so he left the Land." Various men have been suggested for the one who "left the land," ranging from such improbable ones as George Gould and Lieutenant Hunt to more likely figures, such as Samuel Bowles and the Reverend Charles Wadsworth; but the friend who taught her "Immortality" can almost certainly be identified as Benjamin F. Newton. As a young law clerk in Edward Dickinson's office, he served a two-year apprenticeship before starting his own practice in Worcester. Emily later referred to him as a "gentle, yet grave Preceptor, [who taught] me what to read, what authors to admire, what was most grand or beautiful in nature, and that sublimer lesson, a faith in things unseen, and in a life again, nobler, and much more blessed." These tributes acknowledge a profound and far-reaching debt. It must have been Newton who expressed surprise that she had never read Lydia Maria Child's somewhat liberal *Letters from New York*. Newton smuggled this and other radical books past her conservative father. After reading Child's book, Emily exclaimed "This then is a book! And there are more of them!" Reared on a scanty diet of the Bible, standard school classics, and the law-centered library of her father, she must have regarded Newton's broad knowledge of contemporary literature and religious movements as miraculous. His most important gift was a copy of Emerson's poems. Here and in later books by Emerson Emily found dynamic expression of her deepest feelings about the importance of the inner life. Emerson's stress on personal experience over tradition and insistence on self-reliance and the theory of Compensation confirmed her own experimental attitudes. Though none of Emerson's broader social doctrines or optimistic views of human destiny were hers, his Transcendental ideas profoundly affected her. And his concept of the poet "seer" who created new thought and molded souls stirred her poetic ambition.

Newton had already encouraged those ambitions and once told her that she would become a poet. His sympathetic guidance continued during the last years of his life in Worcester, when she first began to write poetry. His death in March of 1853 came as a shattering blow (despite his gentle warning in a final letter), raising again the eternal dilemma of her life, the relation of death to immortality. Later she said that his death stopped all her writing for years. Their relationship was hardly a romantic one, since Newton married soon after leaving Amherst; nevertheless, it remains another example of Emily's strong attachment to an older man that eventually settled into a master-pupil relationship. In Newton she found for the first time a friend with whom she dared to share her inner thoughts and experiences. His encouragement and intellectual stimulus came at the crucial moment of her emergence from school and childhood, while his early death etched clearly upon her soul the tragedy of loss and the frustration of death. As George Whicher has speculated, Newton might be the man referred to in the final lines of her poem, "Your riches—taught me—Poverty," concerning the sudden recognition of a beauty and value now gone.

In general, Emily's life after returning from Mount Holyoke was a satisfying one. The daily round of household activities and the "pestilence" of cleaning occupied much time. Emily shone as the bread and cake baker of the family, even winning a second prize in a baking contest at the fall Cattle Show. Within the town the college provided varied intellectual and social attractions: Amherst professors lectured, Emerson delivered a Lyceum talk, and Jennie Lind gave a concert in nearby Northampton. In 1850 Emily was so enthused by the rush of social events that she wrote: "Amherst is alive with fun this winter . . . Sleigh rides are as plenty as people. . . . Parties cant find fun enough—because all the best ones are engaged to attend balls a week beforehand—beaus can be had for the taking—maids smile like the mornings in June—Oh a very great town is this!" And a few days earlier she attended a New Year's party, enjoying the charades, music, and supper so well that she did not get home until two o'clock that morning. George Gould, the lanky editor of the campus monthly, invited her to a candy-pulling and probably served as her first editor by printing one of her fantastic prose valentines. Elbridge Bowdoin, her father's young law partner, loaned her books, and Emily once thanked him with a mock heroic valentine, taunting his bachelorhood when so many Amherst girls were available. Henry Emmons often took her riding, and they exchanged flowers and books while he was in college. Whether any of these friendships were love affairs seems improbable and none gives any realistic basis for the often repeated tales that her father stopped an attempted elopement, causing Emily to enter permanent seclusion.

Like most young girls she rhapsodized about marriage and sentimentally effused about the great happiness and mystery of the union. Undoubtedly the meretricious presentation of love in popular books inspired some of these enthusiasms. One in particular, Ik Marvel's *Reveries of a Bachelor,* so impressed Emily that her disgruntled father denounced it and all similar modern books as being ridiculous. Marvel's book presented the romantic daydreams of a young bachelor, smoking his pipe by an open fire. It covered the range of available emotional subjects from marriage to immortality with a somewhat frank discussion of love and passion. As Richard Chase has noted in his critical biography of Emily Dickinson, Marvel's vapid portrait of the languishing young girl established a cult of little girl mannerisms which Emily often imitated. She began signing her name "Emilie" and wrote to Austin that she hoped they would never have to grow up. Naturally, the one main outlet from the tensions of maturity was her poetry. In 1853 she wrote Austin, mocking his poetic attempts: "Raised a living muse ourselves, worth the whole nine of them. Up, off, tramp. 'Now Brother Pegasus, I'll tell you what it is—I've been in the habit *myself* of writing a few things, and it rather appears to me that you're getting away with my patent, so you'd better be somewhat careful, or I'll call the police!" Thomas H. Johnson in his *The Poems of Emily Dickinson* is able to date only five poems before 1858, so we know little about her apprenticeship writing. Two of these are mock valentines done in an ornate humorous style, spoofing the receiver. Two poems are conventional lyrics, one on missing Austin and the other a trite account of sailing through the storms of life to the safe harbor of eternity. However, one sent to Sue, "I have a Bird in spring," is an interesting tyro attempt to transmute personal feelings into poetry. Although woodenly phrased with repetitious imagery, the poem conveys her grief over the feared loss of Sue's friendship. Her pathetic search for consolation is touching when she finally states her hope that the flown bird will sing for her again some day.

During the 1850s, while she was still seeking personal under-standing and sympathetic friendships, no new relationship meant more than her affection for Sue Gilbert. If Sue's later marriage to Austin and family interests somewhat excluded Emily and if Emily's own possessive demands irritated Sue, they nevertheless remained close friends. Her early letters to Sue are filled with pathetic demands for Sue's affection and her fears that her love will not be returned. Yet Emily could view her emotional excesses with wry detachment: "In thinking of those I love, my reason is all gone from me, and I do fear sometimes that I must make a hospital for the hopelessly in-sane, and chain me up there such times, so I wont injure you." Any relationship with the volatile and sharp-tongued Sue was bound to be tempestuous, and Emily was continually hurt by Sue's aloofness. Ultimately Emily perceived that Sue's friendship could never be the perfect bond she had once romantically envisioned.

Other important friendships which Emily formed in the 1850s were with Josiah Holland, the literary editor of the Springfield *Re-publican*, and with his wife, Elizabeth. Though a popular writer and later founder of *Scribner's Monthly*, Josiah was completely indiffer-ent to Emily's poetic attempts. In fact, he remarked that her verses were too ethereal and not suitable for publication. However, Emily's first visit to the Hollands' Springfield home remained a treasured memory. She never forgot their warm family relationship nor their open worship of God as a friendly, loving creator. Mrs. Holland most attracted her and for over thirty years she wrote her with a frankness and depth that were given to few other correspondents. Emily entrusted to Mrs. Holland the task of addressing and forward-ing her letters to the Reverend Charles Wadsworth during the 1870s.

Such was her life until the middle 1850s—outwardly normal and filled with new friendships. The revival that converted her father and Sue passed her by; she rarely attended church and, when she did, she remarked that sermons on doubt most attracted her. She referred to herself as quaint and old-fashioned and took the first hesitant steps toward complete seclusion by refusing to go from home unless forced. Perhaps the shock of Newton's death had oc-casioned this desire for solitude. At any rate Emily was increasingly jealous of her limited privacy. She kept in touch with the outside world through correspondence, constantly redrafting letters and lav-ishing care upon their style to create notable touches of originality and wit. Of two visitors she wrote: "They had been *taking a walk*. I think any sentiment must be consecrated by an interview in the mud. There would be certainly, a correspondence in *depth*." The woman was changing, slowly moving toward the love crisis whose white heat was to forge her untempered spirit.

So many impossible and exaggerated stories have been fabricated about her love crisis that one almost despairs of ever identifying the man. Perhaps Austin's remark that Emily was often in love and responded emotionally to many men should always be kept in mind. Nevertheless, her letters, poetry, and final appeal to Higginson indicate some climactic emotional experience during 1860-62. The pattern of her love crisis, so sensitively presented in Theodora Ward's *The Capsule of the Mind,* can be fully examined without reference to any one figure. Reading the poems and letters chronologically from the late 1850s to 1865, one finds a detailed record of a growing emotional attachment. Fed by impossible hopes and increasing erotic desire, this passion burned most intensely at a dramatic summer meeting—only to be extinguished by sudden separation. During the succeeding desolate months, she strove to mend the charred bits of her shattered emotions. Gradually she accepted the loss and began to analyze the experience with surprising detachment. In the final stage, personal renunciation was transformed into a spiritual triumph.

Investigating this general movement more deeply, one sees an obvious change from the early sentimental love lyrics to a growing awareness of a powerful male influence. Gradually there emerges one dominant figure who so devastates her being that images of shipwreck, drowning, and suicide fill the poems. This despairing need is gradually replaced by an exulting surge of emotional fulfillment that is openly erotic as in "Come slowly—Eden!" and "Wild Nights— Wild Nights!" Also in the late 1850s the first of her three "Master" letters was written. These were drafts of three passionately phrased letters all addressed to an unknown recipient called the Master. The first, more general and normal in tone, grieves over the illness of the Master, talks about their separation, and envisions their future meeting in eternity. Her deeper emotional awakening is imaginatively portrayed by a group of marriage lyrics, celebrating her new love status. Other poems deal with a tense final meeting where the lovers talk in a room, walk in her garden, and finally separate. "There came a Day at Summer's full" describes the momentary ecstasy of this meeting and the pathos of parting. It concludes with her trust that after death their love would be culminated by a spiritual marriage. Scores of poems handle this moment of renunciation: "I got so I could take his name," "I Rose—because He sank," and "I cannot live with You." More frightening are the poems dealing with a loss of conscious control and plunge into an unknown abyss of despair. One of the most graphic, "I felt a Funeral, in my Brain," records the soul's final moments of consciousness and its terrible life struggle after the shattering separation from the body. As Theodora Ward comments: "The extraordinary clarity with which she was able to record the experience shows that she did not pass beyond the border of sanity, for the insane cannot explain themselves; but there must have been a period when it was only with the greatest difficulty that she could withstand the disintegrating forces that assailed her." Now her poems explored every conceivable variation of pain, fear, misery, and loss that the human spirit can endure. One of her greatest, "After great pain, a formal feeling comes," compares the after-effects of pain to the slow numbing process of freezing to death. In another poem, "They say that 'Time assuages,'" she defiantly asserts that real suffering increases rather than diminishes with the passage of time. She was literally struggling to save her sanity, and the staggering output of three hundred and sixty-six poems in 1862, her frantic letters to Bowles, and two searing Master drafts show her wavering critically near mental chaos. The abandoned passion of the second Master letter reveals the agony of a disturbed soul:

> I am older—tonight, Master—but the love is the same—so are the moon and the crescent. If it had been God's will that I might breathe where you breathed—and find the place—myself—at night—if I (can) never forget that I am not with you—and that sorrow and frost are nearer than I—if I wish with a might I cannot repress— that mine were the Queen's place. . . . What would you do with me if I came 'in white?' Have you the little chest to put the Alive—in? I want to see you more—Sir—than all I wish for in this world—and the wish—altered a little—will be my only one—for the skies.

As her poems attest, this intense examination of personal grief transcended its particular limits to become a universal account of any human soul that has suffered and endured.

The pendulum swings upward with the gradual acceptance of the pain and realization of its spiritual value. The fleshly lover merges into the Divine and she glories in her renunciation. Poems like "Title divine—is mine" and "Mine—by the Right of White Election" specify her return to a normal life. The journey back was difficult as the specter of eternal loneliness and nagging doubts about the merit of her rejection tortured her. The emotional strain had so ravaged her nervous system that she suffered a physical breakdown in 1864. A long convalescence under doctor's care, during which time she was forbidden to read or to see friends, and her diminished creative drive—only thirty-six poems in 1866 and ten in 1867—indicated that the crisis was past. The exhausted patient slowly recuperated after a particularly painful and near mortal operation. Now the great chapters of anguish and loss were finally closed and she entered fully into her white seclusion.

The identification of her lover has beguiled biographers and readers for generations, but his identity still remains uncertain. However, the Reverend Charles Wadsworth, whose death on April 1, 1882, caused her to comment, "Love has but one Date—'The first of April' 'Today, Yesterday, and Forever,'" is most generally considered to be the man. Their love affair, if it can be called that, was hardly a conventional one. According to what is known, they met only three or four times during their entire lives. The conjectured first meeting probably occurred in March 1855, after Emily visited her father, then a Congressman in Washington. On her journey home she stayed in Philadelphia for two weeks. Wadsworth was pastor of the Arch Street Presbyterian Church in that city, a nationally known preacher whose sermons packed his church. Though he was not an original thinker, the sheer conviction of his orthodox beliefs combined with his moral intensity produced dramatic effects on his hearers. At this time he was forty-four, happily married and, despite his fame, a shy, scholarly man. He so feared public adulation that he entered and left his pulpit without meeting the congregation. She must have heard one of his sermons, and the poem, "He fumbles at your Soul," was possibly a record of this experience. Emily must have experienced an instant rapport and sensed beneath his pulpit manner the same troubling currents that coursed in her own soul. Later she referred to him as "a Dusk Gem, born of troubled Waters, astray in any Crest below," and compared him to Christ as the man of sorrows. She received a copy of his sermons, and they must have exchanged letters since he arranged to meet her in March of 1860 when he was visiting friends in Northampton. Though the details of this encounter may later have been partially dramatized, we can surmise what ardent hopes and explosive tensions charged this initial Amherst meeting. In one of her Master letters she says: "I heard of a thing called 'Redemption'—which rested men and women. You remember I asked you for it—you gave me something else. I forgot the Redemption [in the Redeemed—I did'nt tell you for a long time, but I knew you had altered me—I] and was tired—no more." One possible reading for this is that she originally approached this Master seeking the spiritual guidance that a minister might give, but that her emotional response to his human, personal qualities blinded the spiritual. (In the earliest Master letter there is a specific reference to its being Sunday, as if that would interest the recipient.) What happened at the meeting is uncertain. When she saw his mourning band, as George Whicher indicated, she might have possibly felt that Wadsworth's wife rather than his mother had died and that he was coming to claim her. However, it is difficult to believe that Wadsworth, securely married and most scrupulous, would have instigated a love affair or even understood the nature of her frantic hopes and idealized devotion. Certainly his one extant letter to her indicates little more than a solicitous pastoral concern for some trial she bears. It reveals no deep knowledge of her problem and he even misspells her name with an "e" instead of an "i."

Still, he could have been the force behind her poetic explosion, the figure who provided the spiritual and emotional affinity for which she had been starving. The most intense crisis in her life, "the terror" she felt since September 1861, coincided with her sure knowledge of Wadsworth's intended departure for a new pulpit in Calvary, California. Significantly, the name Calvary now appears prominently in the poems. She calls herself a queen of Calvary, dwells on unfulfilled passion, and after an earthly separation imagines a triumphant spiritual reunion. Her symbolic use of white clothing occurred at this time, as did her final withdrawal into seclusion. Seemingly she mastered her distraught emotions and sublimated her personal tensions with a creative outburst, writing over a thousand poems from 1858 to 1866. And only two weeks before Wadsworth's departure she wrote her first note to Higginson, in what must have been a desperate attempt to obtain some relief from her loss as well as critical comment on the mass of poems she was writing.[1]

With a private poet like Emily Dickinson, biography often provides the key to the complete understanding of a poem. Note, for example, how much biography adds to the haunting lyric "My life

[1] Richard B. Sewall in *The Lyman Letters* presents a new excerpt from one of Emily Dickinson's letters relating to her eye trouble: "Some years ago I had a woe, the only one that ever made me tremble. It was a shutting out of all the dearest ones of time, the strongest friends of the soul—BOOKS." Sewall compares this quotation to the famous passage in the April, 1862 letter to Higginson which reads: "I had a terror—since September—I could tell to none." Usually this "terror" allusion has been related to Dickinson's emotional crisis. However, Sewall links the two passages together by their similar phrasing and ideas and argues that the "terror" remark alludes to Dickinson's fear of losing her ability to read. This interpretation appears limited, because the excerpt itself is undated and because Dickinson's serious eye trouble occurred late in 1863 and 1864—two years beyond the "terror" of September, 1861.

closed twice before its close." The poem clearly states that she has suffered the equivalent of physical death by two previous losses. Now she wonders if Immortality (God or fate) has still another treasure to offer. Biographically the two losses could be Newton and Wadsworth—her separation from Newton by physical death and the deprivation of Wadsworth by geographical distance and moral barriers. Prophetically she wonders about a possible third figure (and one actually came in the 1870s with her Indian summer love for Judge Otis Lord). The second stanza concisely summarizes the overwhelming sense of desolation that these losses occasioned. Parting reveals heaven, since its ecstasy rivals paradise, besides emphasizing the soul's dependency upon heaven for future happiness. At the same time the experience of hell comes in the anguish of separation.

Some critics have conjectured another interview before Wadsworth's departure, but there is no evidence for such a meeting. We know nothing about their correspondence in the 1860s, but it is significant that when Wadsworth's return from California was announced she invited Higginson to her home, saying that he had once saved her life and she wanted to thank him in person. Her emotions were now mastered and she could examine her former passion with comparative objectivity. Love was never to poetically inspire her again, and very few of the two hundred poems she wrote in the early 1870s dealt with an emotional attachment. During this time she corresponded with Wadsworth by having the Hollands forward her letters to his Philadelphia home. In 1880 he paid her a surprise visit. She was in her garden when Vinnie told her that Wadsworth wanted to see her. Emily asked him why he had not announced his visit, so she might have prepared for it. Speaking like an "Apparition," he replied: "Because I did not know it myself. I stepped from my Pulpit to the Train." When she asked how long a journey it was: " 'Twenty years' said he with inscrutable roguery." At one point in their talk he commented that he was liable to die at any time.

Wadsworth's death came as a shock to Emily, though they had seen each other only twice in over twenty years. Despite an announcement in the papers, Vinnie did not read about it for over a week. When she discovered it, she rushed to tell Emily, who had been living with the news and who could only respond: "How *can* the sun shine, Vinnie?" Soon afterward, Emily initiated her correspondence with the Clark brothers, Wadsworth's friends, and cherished every bit of personal information they furnished about his life, family, final hours, and religious thoughts. The letters she wrote them in the next four years reveal how uninformed she was about his personal life. These facts support the conclusion that most of the passion and intimacy of the relationship existed in Emily's imagination and that Wadsworth probably never suspected her emotional ordeal. Still, the relationship remained the most important of her life, and it taught her, imaginatively at least, all she needed to know of passion and suffering.

Unless we include the outside possibility of an unknown figure or try to force people like Henry Emmons or John Graves into the role, the only other logical choice for Emily's lover was Samuel Bowles. Many critics have so considered him, and his age, personality, and closeness to the Dickinsons and the intimate letters Emily wrote him allow this interpretation. Emily's response to him was open and at times ecstatic. She praised his vibrant personality and wrote that he had "the most triumphant Face out of Paradise—probably because [he was] there constantly, instead of ultimately." As editor of the Springfield *Republican* for over thirty years, Bowles transformed that small town weekly into a daily of national importance, bringing to it pages the verve that characterized his high-spirited personality. Though he wrote popular travel books, achieved political importance, and knew his paper to be one of America's finest, he found only in his friendship with Austin Dickinson the needed release from office tensions and a strained home relationship. By 1860 the two households were intimate, although Bowles's invalid wife Mary felt eclipsed by Sue's wit and exciting personality—one of the many instances of her jealous attitude about Bowles's attractiveness to women.

Bowles was on friendly terms with Emily, but the greatest intensity in their correspondence came during the fall and winter of 1861-62. The open appeals for sympathy and the anguished, disordered tone of Emily's letters closely resemble the two most revealing Master letters. In the fall Bowles was recuperating from an illness in Northampton and frequently rode over to Austin's Amherst home. On one of these visits Emily sent him a note saying that, although she cared for him, something bothered her and she could not see him. The real cause of this withdrawal is not known, but she ended the letter by comparing herself to the Marchioness in Dickens' *The Old Curiosity Shop* and Bowles to Dick Swiveller, who later married the Marchioness. The series of letters that followed during the winter show her increasing concern for Bowles's health and apprehension about his coming trip to Europe. The feverish ardor and hidden allusions in the letters suggest Bowles's awareness of her emotional distress and allow an interpretation of "lover."

One letter, dated January 11, asks cryptically if he is willing to help her in some unnamed distress. Critics have suggested that she was asking him to forward a letter to Wadsworth or sending him a poem. The reference remains obscure, but she clearly indicates her need of assistance and hopes to repay his kindness some day. An even more disturbing letter followed: "If I amaze[d] your kindness—My love is my only apology. To the people of 'Chillon'—this—is enoug[h] I have met—no othe[rs.] Would you ask less for your *Queen*—M[r] Bowles?" Her reference to Queen and an illegible word that seems to be "Daisy" significantly echo similar phrases used in the Master letters. In another letter she enclosed one of her most intense Bride poems, "Title divine—is mine," cautioning him on his honor to tell no one. Is she indirectly telling him of her great passion by poetically declaring that she realizes their love is hopeless and that her role must be that of a wife in spirit? Or does it refer to someone else? The next letter, perhaps in answer to his own harassed questions about what the poem meant, enclosed the poem "Through the strait pass of suffering," which triumphantly affirms her moral survival after a nightmare of temptation. One letter uses the fiction of Austin's name to declare her affection, while the poem "Victory comes late" comprises another. Repeatedly she expresses her gratitude for his understanding and sympathy, while also openly courting his pity and emotional response. In her last letter before his departure for Europe she pleads for a final visit. It was less than a week after he sailed that she wrote her first letter to Higginson. In her second letter she mentions a "terror—since September" (Bowles's illness had been that fall) and her tutor who has "left the land" (Bowles's recent departure to Europe fits perfectly, while Wadsworth did not sail for California until May 1).

Throughout Bowles's stay in Europe Emily's letters inquire about his health and stress her impatience for his return. Yet, when he finally returned in November she refused to see him. Another letter somewhat confusedly argues that she prizes "the Grace [her awareness of his spiritual reality]—superior to the Sign [his actual physical presence]" and that she does not want to usurp his time with Austin. She then says that he must understand, for "Few absences could seem so wide as your's." Succeeding critics have been no less baffled than Bowles must have been by her actions. Whether the undoubted strain of seeing him after her renunciation was too much or whether she was trying to test his affection can probably never be determined. Since she increasingly repeated that pattern with other friends, this withdrawal might have been a stratagem to avoid debilitating encounters. Nevertheless, their relationship became decidedly impersonal in the next few years. By 1863 Bowles joked about Emily's actions, calling her "Queen Recluse" and satirizing her precious mannerisms by asking, "Is it really true that they ring 'Old Hundred' and 'Aleluia' [sic] perpetually, in heaven—ask her?" These were hardly the remarks of a man in love or one who had been through a deeply moving personal experience. It was not until after the death of her father that their letters resumed an intimate tone and their exchange returned to the easy one of old friends. At Bowles's death Emily frankly displayed her great affection, and her letters to Mary Bowles and Maria Whitney, another close personal friend of Bowles, show a profound appreciation of his nature. Ambiguous and baffling as their relationship was, her attachment to Bowles remains an important one for understanding her love crisis.

The complexities of anyone's emotional life are difficult to unravel, and with an elusive, many-faceted personality like Emily Dickinson the hidden areas may never be fully illuminated. Whether Wadsworth or Bowles or some still unknown person was her imagined or actual lover is less important than the fact that her passionate response to this figure occasioned some of the finest lyrics in the entire range of American poetry.

3

A POET'S MIND

THE PASSION and deprivation that tempered her soul also matured her distinct personality and ultimately formed the poet. As she remarked to Higginson, she could tell no one about her psychological fears; and so she sang "as the Boy does by the Burying Ground— because I am afraid." To her Norcross cousins, Louise and Frances, she said that she sang off "Charnel steps. Every day life feels mightier, and what we have the power to be, more stupendous." In both these remarks she stressed that poetry grew directly out of her personal experiences and served as an outlet for frustrated emotions. Coupled with this is her exhilaration in experiencing life and poetically recording its sensations. In writing about these feelings the prose often changes openly into poetry, as in this letter to Mrs. Holland about her present separation from her husband:

> Am told that fasting gives to food marvellous Aroma, but by birth a Bachelor, disavow Cuisine.
> Meeting is well worth parting. How kind in some to die, adding *impatience* to the rapture of our thought of Heaven!
>
> > As by the dead we love to sit—
> > Become so wondrous dear—
> >
> > . . . .
> >
> > In broken Mathematics
> > We estimate our prize
> > *Vast*, in it's *fading* ratio
> > To our penurious eyes.
>
> I had rather you lived nearer—I would like to touch you. Pointed attentions from the Angels, to two or three I love, make me sadly jealous.

Here the thought in the prose, so close to poetry, finally becomes a poem, intensifying Mrs. Holland's separation to include Emily's sense of deprivation. As we have seen throughout her letters to Bowles, it is impossible to separate the prose from the poetry, for actual poems often conveyed her deepest feelings. The question of why she wrote is perhaps answered by asking why she lived and experienced all areas of life so intensely. In a sense her poetry preserved her individuality and provided the needed release for yearnings that threatened her balance. With a daring skill she transformed personal losses into imperishable lyrics of self-exploration. Her isolation and suffering developed in her a habit of introspection and a fascination with the hidden areas of the soul. Like another contrary New Englander, Henry David Thoreau, she too traveled "widely" within the confines of a small town. Rather than escape life, she fronted it on the most trying battleground—in her own spirit—and mastered it through her art. In more ways than one her poetry was her triumphant "letter to the World/That never wrote to Me."

Immediately comes the question, why was this letter never sent and why did she remain a private poet? Framing an answer is difficult, but an obvious one is indicated above. So much of her inner soul was exposed in these poems and so much did they constitute an intimate spiritual biography that having them published was unthinkable. Perhaps sharing hundreds of them with close friends and sympathetic literary outsiders like Higginson was all she dared. However, this is a superficial answer and her countless poems and remarks on fame indicate her desire to be known and published. In response to a note from her sister-in-law, Sue, praising her poetry, she remarked that she treasured Sue's comments and hoped to make the Dickinson family proud of her someday. Her poems on fame reveal a similar hunger for recognition, though by 1863 this is assuaged by the inner assurance that creation done for immortality's sake does not need time's fickle rewards.

Still, she published or others published seven poems during her lifetime. Excluding "Some keep the Sabbath going to Church" and "Success," all of them appeared in the Springfield *Republican*. In an early letter to Higginson she commented: "Two Editors of Journals came to my Father's House, this winter—and asked me for my Mind —and when I asked them 'Why,' they said I was penurious—and they, would use it for the World." By this she can only mean that Bowles and Holland asked for some of her poetry. Yet, when "I taste a liquor never brewed" was published in 1861 the first stanza was considerably altered to insure perfect rhyme. Her original verse read:

> I taste a liquor never brewed—
> From Tankards scooped in Pearl—
> Not all the Frankfort Berries
> Yield such an Alcohol!

But the last two lines were printed as:

> Not Frankfort berries yield the sense
> Such a delirious whirl.

So the delicate blend of "l" in "pearl" and "alcohol," and the interplay of "a" and "o" sounds were destroyed for the sake of conventional rhyme. Later when her poem "The Snake" was published with an editor's punctuation that separated the third and fourth lines, she exasperatedly wrote to Higginson that not only was the poem published without her permission, but that the editor's incorrect punctuation changed its meaning. Indeed Bowles could only comment about the poem: "How did that girl ever know that a boggy field wasn't good for corn?" His own literary taste ran to the hardy adventure narratives of Bret Harte and Joaquin Miller; similarly, Holland favored the sentimental, bland verses of the genteel writers. Neither of them thought her poems publishable.

It is no wonder then that, when she turned to another literary figure, Thomas Wentworth Higginson, and received his advice not to publish, she furtively withdrew. Unable to solve the problem of publication and artistic integrity, she rationalized that her "Barefoot-Rank" was better. Her final position, one that ultimately despaired of ever publishing her poems in their intended form or finding a sympathetic audience, was given in the poem "Publication—is the Auction," where she said that publication was the exposure of one's mind for a price. Though an extreme position, and perhaps an unjustified one in the light of what was actually published in the late nineteenth century, this attitude hardened into an unshakable determination never to publish. Her only other published poem after 1866 was obtained by the clever stratagems of Helen Hunt Jackson. Even then, obtaining her permission took over two years of maneuvering and probably succeeded because Emily was so anxious to keep Helen Hunt Jackson's exciting literary friendship. Her few tentative experiences with the publishing world so seared her sensitive nature that limited poetic exchange with intimate friends had to remain sufficient.

When one considers the deplorable public taste of the time and measures the neglect of Whitman's *Leaves of Grass* and the ridicule of Poe's "jingles" against the fame of Longfellow and weaker writers like N. P. Willis and Mrs. Sigourney, it appears she chose the right course. A comparison of her poem on a child's death with Mrs. Sigourney's famous "Death of an Infant" demonstrates Emily Dickinson's achievement and indicates why her verses might not have found a public then. Here is Sigourney's poem:

> Death found strange beauty on that cherub brow,
> And dashed it out,—There was a tint of rose
> On cheek and lip,—he touched the veins with ice,
> And the rose faded;—forth from those blue eyes
>
> There spake a wishful tenderness,—a doubt
> Whether to grieve or sleep, which Innocence
> Alone can wear. With ruthless haste he bound
> The silken fringes of their curtaining lids
>
> Forever;—there had been a murmuring sound,
> With which the babe would claim its mother's ear,
> Charming her even to tears. The Spoiler set
> His seal of silence.—But there beamed a smile
>
> So fixed and holy from that marble brow,—
> Death gazed, and left it there;—he dared not steal
> The signet-ring of Heaven.

Her theme, the triumph of innocence over death itself, is presented by the most hackneyed imagery, "cherub brow," "silken fringes," and "tint of rose," and awkwardly phrased. How, for example, does a brow beam a smile? Death is conventionally described as the spoiler, the evil, blackhearted villain whose ruthless attacks are thwarted by pristine goodness. Throughout, the appeal relies on the stock images of the sorrowing mother and the helpless child and falls into bathos, eulogizing the child's incredible perfection. One could never imagine this infant abstraction as an ordinary child sitting in a high chair or dirtying his knees on a kitchen floor.

Emily Dickinson's poem handles a similar theme:

> She lay as if at play
> Her life had leaped away—
> Intending to return—
> But not so soon—
>
> Her merry Arms, half dropt—
> As if for lull of sport—
> An instant had forgot—
> The Trick to start—
>
> . . . .
>
> Her Morning at the door—
> Devising, I am sure—
> To force her sleep—
> So light—so deep—

This poem gains sympathy not by lingering over silken fringes and marble brows but by presenting the girl's vitality and elusiveness. The child's light movement, "play" approach to life, and whimsical nature bring genuine pathos, mocking death's heavy finality. This effect of lightness and activity is developed by the subtle interplay of meter, rhyme, and imagery. The poem's meter—trimeter with ending dimeter feet—is unusually short and quick moving; the first lines contain an internal rhyme ("lay" and "play"), openly stress the "l" sound, and even draw out "so" into "soon" to end the stanza; and most of the words are simple, with only a few longer than two syllables. All of this perfectly catches a child's delight in repetitive devices and rapid movement.

The first view of the girl emphasizes her hesitant "as if" quality, which guides the whole poetic movement. Her death is not a solemn, ponderous thing, but such an abrupt surprise that it cannot be accepted as final. The next two stanzas further develop this "play" image by accentuating her "sport" and "trick" qualities and by the somewhat trite, though appropriately childlike, images of "merry arms" and "dancing eyes." These conventional phrases are freshened by the girl's naïve belief that life is only a special knack or magic key, temporarily lost, but which can be easily found again to start the toy body. The last stanza reworks the nature-in-mourning tradition of classical elegy with a Dickinson twist. Morning is particularly "hers," since its dawn quality reflects her personality, and morning becomes a playmate who is puzzled and a bit irritated by her sleeping. So poutingly it stands outside the door, resolving "to force her sleep." The word "force" darkens the final lines (as the pun of mourning in "morning" catches the paradox of life and death's close connection) and hints at nature's inexorable rule over man's mortality. Though her sleep is seen as light and temporary, the poem ends with the heaviness of "deep"; while the exact rhyming couplet and repeated dimeter lines break the earlier pattern to stress the finality of death. In this poem a skillful handling of imagery and detail bypasses the mawkish sentimentality of Sigourney's poem to develop true pathos.

By the time Emily Dickinson was published in 1890 the public was better able to appreciate her quality and her work achieved a surprising success. However, despite her popularity in the 1890s, her Bohemian appeal in the 1920s, and recent critical acclaim, she was a private poet, and her poetry remains difficult for many readers. Her particular cast of mind and her predominant themes have to be understood before one fully appreciates her poetic achievement.

Though she was not a philosopher, nor even a consistent thinker, she strikingly illuminated hidden recesses in the human soul. Unlike most other American poets, she was religiously oriented. Even a cursory glance at her themes reveals an extreme preoccupation with the effect of death, the nature of the soul, the problems of immortality, the possibility of faith, and the reality of God. Certainly in the sense that she sought the essential moral truths veiled behind material appearances and strove to experience and perceive the Divine force (or as she phrased it "Circumference") she was mystically inclined.

Although later influenced by Transcendentalism, she was reared in an orthodox tradition where biblical truths were couched in Calvinistic terms. Nor did she ever eradicate the hard core of these beliefs from her philosophy. The basic Calvinistic approach, as rigidly taught in the seventeenth century, maintained that man was depraved and conditioned to evil by original sin and that he was utterly dependent on God for any good he might accomplish. Further, this God was absolute and arbitrary, freely electing to save or to damn. Knowing men's fate beforehand, God predestined the course of their lives. Allied to this was the concept of irresistible grace; that is, once given it could not be refused or lost. In the legal terminology of the Puritan covenant the key words were sanctification and justification. One was "justified" when God gave him the grace necessary for a good life and "sanctified" when he continued to prove his election by living an acceptable Christian life. Undergirding this whole complex structure was the universality of the moral law that God directed all men's acts.

In nineteenth-century Amherst these Calvinistic beliefs were not so rigidly enforced, and anyone who felt so moved could declare his own justification and become one of the elect. There was none of the searching personal examination and period of trial that Jonathan Edwards fought for—only a willingness to attend church regularly and superficially to manifest a moral life. Even this was too much for Emily Dickinson. Openly envying the serenity of converted Christians, she still found herself a rebel and quite mystified by the process of conversion and the doctrine of election. During the 1850s she stopped attending church and noted that all her family were religious but herself. By this she meant that she could not accept the harsh dogmas of innate depravity, arbitrary election, and predestination, or revere the Bible as true history and the only moral guide for man. In other words, she rejected all that made man insignificant and helpless before the crushing force of God. In many poems, like

"Abraham to kill him" and "Of God we ask one favor," she satirizes the orthodox belief that all men are responsible for the sin of the first parents. Continually she pictures God the father as an aloof tyrant, indifferently dealing out blind punishments, unresponsive to prayer, and unconcerned about human suffering. In one poem, "Heavenly Father—take to thee," she ironically comments on God's duplicity for at once creating men with original sin and then condemning them for fulfilling their nature. Her favorite biblical figures were the arch-angel Gabriel, who brought God's mysterious tidings to earth, Moses, who was denied entrance to the Holy Land for some minor infraction of God's rules, and Jacob, who wrestled with God and won. For Christ she had greater affection, though it was marked by a cautious ambivalence that emphasized his human rather than divine qualities. She once wrote: "When Jesus tells us about his Father, we distrust him. When he shows us his Home, we turn away, but when he confides to us that he is 'acquainted with Grief,' we listen, for that also is an Acquaintance of our own." If she could not accept conventional religion, she still retained an unshakable trust in God's actual reality and continually re-examined older, fundamental concepts like the Trinity, resurrection, hell, angels, and immortality. Throughout her life the ultimate mystery of immortality perplexed and intrigued her. Especially in her later years the problem obsessed her, but she remained a doubter till her death.

In the main her poetry typified the moral earnestness of the old Puritans, with their confidence that the human soul could overcome imperfection through struggle and self-discipline. She clearly perceived that the soul's inner reality contained true value, not the external world of nature. Like Thoreau she felt that each individual must strip life down to its bare bones and savor for himself its sweet marrow or gag on its bitterness. Her exhilaration with the process of living remained uniquely her own, and she repeatedly exclaimed: "I find ecstasy in living—the mere sense of living is joy enough." Part of this intensity developed from the lonely struggle to preserve her integrity and the continual testing of her soul in the crucible of pain. She was a particularly introspective poet, interested in probing self-analysis to the exclusion of any outside issues. Her isolation from contemporary affairs was total, and the major historical event during her lifetime, the Civil War, she passed over with only a few incidental references to soldiers and Lincoln's re-election. This unconcern was epitomized by an aside to Mrs. Holland about a coming Presidential election: "Before I write to you again, we shall have a new Czar—Is the Sister a Patriot? 'George Washington was the

Father of his Country'—'George Who?' That sums all Politics to me
—but then I love the Drums, and they are busy now." Not even
Thoreau was able to keep this distance from sectional and political
events.

She constantly wrote about the nature of Compensation—that we
learn by experiencing the opposite of what we desire—though she
never accepted Emerson's belief in the harmonious correspondence
of man and nature. In much the same manner as modern philosophers
like Tillich she viewed man as an estranged, beleaguered creature
who is put under continual stress without any certainty that his
pain will merit salvation or that he will even understand the meaning of life. Her short poem "Success" exemplifies this phase of her
thought:

> Success is counted sweetest
> By those who ne'er succeed.
> To comprehend a nectar
> Requires sorest need.
>
> Not one of all the purple Host
> Who took the Flag today
> Can tell the definition
> So clear of Victory
>
> As he defeated—dying—
>
> . . . .

The poet Richard Wilbur in a recent essay has succinctly pointed
out that the poem not only shows her belief in the laws of opposition,
that loss enables one to understand victory, but that defeat is superior, since an achieved victory soon loses its value. For Emily
Dickinson, desire best defines a thing; anticipation and search are
all. Desire allows the intellect and imagination to comprehend (note
she does not say to taste) a nectar, something precious and given
only to the gods. By understanding the essence of an object one
transcends its temporary physical reality to possess its universal
core. "Success" is one of many definition poems usually starting
"Experience is," "Renunciation is," "Love is," "Ecstasy is." In them
she relentlessly tried to express the meaning of intangible objects and
emotional states, to determine their various properties, and to understand their relation to the human soul. Remarks like "Each of us
gives or takes heaven in corporeal person, for each of us has the skill
of life" reveal her unique blending of Calvinism and Transcendentalism. Perhaps she only rationalized losses into gains, but her experimental turn of mind usually perceived different sides to each event.

With this double vision she often embraced contradictory positions and moved easily from the physical to the spiritual.

Relying on her own experience, she instinctively perceived that the spirit transcended the physical and that moments of insight that temporarily approach the divine were possible. These mystic experiences were explored in poems dealing with ecstasy, transport, awe, immortality, and circumference. What exactly she meant by her remark that "the Bible dealt with the Centre, not with the Circumference" is not clear, but it was intimately related to her feeling that the poet possesses a God-like creative power. "Circumference" implied an extension outward to include something larger than one's self, a heightened consciousness of the eternal, which is just beyond finite man. In a sense, circumference was an experience of grace; somewhat like Jonathan Edwards' description of his mystical conversion in a "Personal Narrative": "It was a sweet, and gentle, and holy majesty; and also a majestic meekness; an awful sweetness; a high, and great, and holy gentleness." One lived for these moments of insight, for life was only a widening of our areas of understanding, an expansion of circumference into the nature of God. However, as man's perception, being dependent on the outside physical world, was necessarily limited, so this vision remained transitory. Also she believed that the "supernatural is only the natural disclosed" and continually wondered if heaven could possess all the beauty found on earth.[1]

Pragmatically Emily Dickinson felt that nature, God, and man were rarely in harmony and that change and flux were more the essence of life than cosmic correspondence. She perceived that the closer one got to this essence the more ambiguous and complex it became. Despite her acceptance of God's reality, she was too much a New England doubter to trust Him or to find satisfaction in nature. Richard Chase in his biography has noted a corollary to these beliefs, holding that Emily Dickinson viewed life as a continual progression from one level to the next until one reached the highest rungs, death and immortality. People with spiritual insight or circumference often achieved a "Queen state," where they arbitrarily ruled over a select kingdom. So her posture in poems like "The Soul selects her own Society" and frequent references to herself as "Queen" or "Empress" had the further significance of a spiritual aristocracy and constituted a secular reworking of the Calvinist doctrine of election.

---

[1] Albert J. Gelpi in his *Emily Dickinson: The Mind of the Poet* has an excellent and extended discussion of the paradoxical elements involved in Emily Dickinson's use of the term "Circumference."

Her staggering creative drive in the 1860s was followed by a period of emotional and artistic exhaustion. During this time her gradual withdrawal from active social life hardened into total seclusion. The problem of her retreat has often been handled as a dramatic renunciation of the world which preserved her soul's integrity and insured her artistic freedom. However, the probable explanation is much less sensational. In the early 1850s she refused to leave her home except for the most pressing social engagements and, considering her close-knit family ties, this was not unusual. By the later 1850s Vinnie and her mother performed even these functions, and she wrote to her Norcross cousins that there were only a few from whom she did not "run away." She was acutely aware of her unusual personality and perplexed by the inability of outsiders to comprehend her thinking. In 1861-62 she began to refuse to see close friends like Bowles. Perhaps it was an attempt to spare her excitable, emotional nature, which so often exploded, leaving her prostrated. She accentuated her isolation by dressing in white, and she developed many striking mannerisms, even receiving visitors while seated behind a slightly opened door. One description of her by a graduating Amherst senior is worth quoting:

> She did not often appear at the companies [socials] given in her father's house, and when she did, she seemed more like an apparition than a reality. At a moment when conversation lagged a little, she would sweep in, clad in immaculate white, pass through the rooms, silently courtseying [sic] and saluting right and left, and sweep out again. . . . She was vacillating in her mental processes and not always interesting, but at times she seemed almost inspired.

By the 1870s her seclusion was absolute. She emphasized her social indifference by remarking to Higginson: "I never thought of conceiving that I could ever have the slightest approach to such a want in all future time . . . I feel that I have not expressed myself strongly enough."

The facts seem clear, but the inner reasons are not so obvious. Certainly the peculiar introspective bent of her mind made her somewhat indifferent to place or society. Then, too, finding time for her creative writing, reading, and correspondence posed a difficult problem. Her father entertained all important town visitors; the calls of close friends were frequent, as were the longer stays of relatives; and, though free of the major tasks of housekeeping and cooking, she still had to perform specific family duties. Only a strict economy with personal activities could glean the precious time she so desperately needed. With frequent visitors and letter exchanges, it was therefore possible for her to keep in touch with the outside world without leaving the home. Because of her sensitive nature, the anticipation and the excitement of visits from close friends often exhausted her. In a sense her retirement was a refuge for her exposed emotions. Also contributing to her withdrawal was her sense of dramatic effect. Within the confines of her home she could maintain the pretense of ruling as an unapproachable queen, importuned by abject subjects to whom she capriciously denied or granted access. So in her own unique manner Emily Dickinson, like Nathaniel Hawthorne, shouted her "No! in Thunder" to a conventional world.

After 1865 Emily severely limited social contacts even with her friends, rarely seeing anyone beyond her immediate home and Austin's family. She once described how her weeks passed: "You ask me if I see any one—Judge Lord was with me a week in October and I talked with Father's Clergyman once, and once with Mr. Bowles. Little—wayfaring acts—comprise my 'pursuits'—and a few moments at night, for Books—after the rest sleep. Candor . . . is the only wile." A neighbor who played the piano for Emily described her as "a pair of great, dark eyes set in a small, pale, delicately chiseled face, and a little body, quaint, simple as a child and wholly unaffected." A group of neighbors to whom she constantly sent flowers and cakes and correspondence with friends like Bowles, Higginson, Lord, Wadsworth, Mrs. Jackson, Maria Whitney, and her Norcross cousins provided sufficient social outlets. To keep these friendships intimate, she wrote over seven hundred known letters in her last twenty years, lavishing time and artistic skill on drafts and redrafts in the hazardous attempt to unfold her mind. Though often filled with personal allusions and tag phrases from her reading, these letters still are thought-provoking and crammed with wit and satire. Leaping from point to point in a characteristic Dickinson shorthand, they dazzle with epigrammatic phrases and salient observations. Of an elderly caller who inquired about buying a house: "I directed her to the cemetery to spare expense of moving"; and of a stern visiting relative: "L goes to Sunderland, Wednesday, for a minute or two; leaves here at 6½—what a fitting hour—and will breakfast the night before; such a smart atmosphere! The trees stand right up straight when they hear her boots, and will bear crockery wares instead of fruit, I fear. She hasn't starched the geraniums yet, but will have ample time, unless she leaves before April."

As noted above, one of the few friendships cultivated in her later years was with Helen Hunt Jackson. Though Mrs. Jackson was born and lived in Amherst during early childhood, she had barely known Emily Dickinson before Higginson showed her some of the poetry. By the early 1870s, when Mrs. Jackson was achieving popular success, she and Emily had become correspondents. Of course, she had no particular effect on Emily's writing or manner of life, but her singular appreciation of the poetry and confidence in its greatness remained the most valued literary acknowledgment Emily ever received. Mrs. Jackson's earliest known letter to Emily expresses a hope that they can become acquainted and concludes: "I have a little manuscript volume with a few of your verses in it—and I read them very often—You are a great poet—and it is a wrong to the day you live in, that you will not sing aloud." After the qualified approval of Higginson and the doubts of Bowles and Holland, this open praise from America's foremost woman writer must have given Emily marked satisfaction. Later personal meetings so deepened their intimacy that Mrs. Jackson was able to use her personal influence in obtaining Emily's brief poem "Success" for a collection of anonymous verse entitled *A Masque of Poets*. The dodges employed by Emily to avoid publication before finally succumbing to Mrs. Jackson's persistence were monumental, but what is important about Mrs. Jackson's efforts and their continued friendship was her recognition of Emily Dickinson's poetic ability. In one of her final letters Mrs. Jackson chastises Emily for hoarding her "portfolios of verses," begs to be made her literary executor, and prophetically remarks: "Surely, after you are what is called 'dead,' you will be willing that the poor ghosts you have left behind, should be cheered and pleased by your verses, will you not?—You ought to be." Unfortunately Mrs. Jackson died before she could be appointed, and also there is no assurance that Emily would have allowed it had she lived.

However, the most important relationship of her later years was the friendship and finally the love of Judge Otis Lord. Eighteen years older than Emily, Judge Lord was an eminent Massachusetts lawyer, happily married and a close friend of Edward Dickinson. Under the shock of her father's death Emily instinctively turned to Lord for sympathy and affection in order to survive the terrible desolation that now filled her life. When Lord's own wife died in 1877 their affection deepened into a mature, satisfying love that was both ardent and complete. One of her letters to Lord shows the frank expression of a secure, passionate attachment:

> My lovely Salem smiles at me. I seek his Face so often—but I have done with guises.
> I confess that I love him—I rejoice that I love him—I thank the

maker of Heaven and Earth—that gave him me to love—the exultation floods me. I cannot find my channel—the Creek turns Sea—at thought of thee.

Will you punish me? "Involuntary Bankruptcy," how could that be Crime?

Incarcerate me in yourself—rosy penalty—threading with you this lovely maze, which is not Life or Death—though it has the intangibleness of one, and the flush of the other—waking for your sake on Day made magical with you before I went.

A series of tender, playful, and passionate letters covered the years until his death in 1884. Thus he became her last master, closing the series of these relationships which had begun with Ben Newton when she was nineteen. But this master surpassed all previous ones and his frank affection sounded untouched emotional depths in her woman's nature. They seriously contemplated marriage and Emily could jokingly refer to herself as his wife, asking if she had his approval. Obviously she had, but the pressures of Lord's ill health and Emily's family obligations prevented an actual marriage. Her life of pain and denial was transformed by this late flowering of mature love, almost as if her tortured struggle had earned her the right to a measure of earthly happiness.

Nevertheless it was with death, not love, that she spent most of her final years. Bowles died in 1878, Holland in 1881, Wadsworth and her mother a year later; while Lord himself suffered a severe stroke that May. The most devastating shock, because it was so unexpected, was the death of her favorite nephew Gilbert at the age of eight in 1883. It profoundly affected both Dickinson households and once again opened the breach between Austin and Sue (and Emily) that only Gilbert's presence had repaired. Her letter of consolation to Sue is a moving expression of just what place the boy held in their lives and indicates how the artist could transform personal anguish into a universal affirmation of human faith:

The Vision of Immortal Life has been fulfilled—
How simply at the last the Fathom comes! The Passenger and not the Sea, we find surprises us—
Gilbert rejoiced in Secrets—
His Life was panting with them—With what menace of Light he cried "Dont tell, Aunt Emily"! Now my ascended Playmate must instruct *me*. Show us, prattling Preceptor, but the way to thee!
He knew no niggard moment—His Life was full of Boon—The Playthings of the Deverish were not so wild as his—
No crescent was this Creature—He traveled from the Full—
Such soar, but never set—

I see him in the Star, and meet his sweet velocity in everything
that flies—His Life was like the Bugle, which winds itself away, his
Elegy an echo—his Requiem ecstasy—

Dawn and Meridian in one.

Wherefore would he wait, wronged only of Night, which he left for
us—

Without a speculation, our little Ajax spans the whole—

Her own nervous collapse a few weeks after Lord's death was the
beginning of a protracted illness from which she died on May 15,
1886. Higginson came for the funeral, read a selection on immortality
from Emily Brontë, and commented that her face was "a wondrous
restoration of youth—she is 54 [55] & looked 30, not a gray hair or
wrinkle, & perfect peace on the beautiful brow." At her neck were a
bunch of violets and Vinnie put two heliotropes by her hand to carry
to Judge Lord. There was no funeral service as the white casket was
simply carried to the cemetery across the fields full of innocents and
buttercups.

The aftermath is literary history, though a publishing footnote
may be appropriate. Emily left instructions that all her papers be
burned and Vinnie faithfully carried out the holocaust until she
came to the hundreds of poems collected in Emily's cherry bureau.
Stunned by such an accumulation, she decided they should be published as a tribute to her sister's genius. The manuscripts ranged
from those in finished form, carefully arranged in small packets, to
those written on scraps of old letters, on the backs of bills, and on
the inside of envelopes. Many of the poems were in roughest work-
sheet form, filled with alternate words and phrases and without any
indication of final preference. Her difficult handwriting and idiosyn-
cratic manner of punctuation and capitalization, coupled with the
complete absence of composition dates for the poems, also created
serious editing problems. Fortunately, over a thousand were written
in ink and carefully gathered in small packets of usually twenty or
more poems in a group. These five or six pages of stationery were
tied together by a thread and when opened could be read like a book.
Although these might easily be deciphered, they were hardly ready
for printing when a naïve Vinnie rushed to Sue demanding that they
promptly be sent off for publication. Sue took the manuscripts, but
delayed so long during the fall and winter that Vinnie precipitously
took the poems back and gave them to Mabel Loomis Todd. The
young wife of an Amherst professor, Mabel Todd had been in Am-

Safe in their Alabas-
ter Chambers -
Untouched by Morning -
And untouched by Noon -
Sleep the meek mem-
bers of the Resurrection
Rafter of Satin - and
Roof of Stone -

Grand go the Years.
In the Crescent - above
them -
Worlds scoop their Arcs.
And Firmaments - row -
Diadems - drop -
And Doges - surrender
Soundless as Dots,
On a Disc of Snow

FACSIMILE OF "SAFE IN THEIR ALABASTER CHAMBERS"

herst only since 1881, but her beauty, personality, and tact had won Vinnie's friendship. Though she never saw Emily, she often played the piano for her hidden listener, and they exchanged notes and poems. Well acquainted with the quality of Emily Dickinson's mind and sincerely affected by the beauty of the poems, she took the difficult job of editing and finally persuaded a begrudging Higginson to co-edit a first collection in 1890. The posthumous publication achieved great popular success. By 1896 over five hundred of the poems had been published in three books and a collection of letters edited. Family quarrels, tangled personal emotions, and lawsuits finally halted systematic printing. Throughout the next fifty years carelessly edited segments of the poetry were randomly printed until *Bolts of Melody* (1945), an edition of nearly seven hundred previously unpublished poems, provided an accurate text. And only in 1955 did Thomas H. Johnson's authoritative edition of her known poems appear.

4

A POET'S PRACTICE

Emerson once defined the function of poetry in "Merlin":

> Its chords should ring as blows the breeze
> Free, peremptory, clear.
> No Jingling serenader's art
>
> . . . .
>
> The kingly bard
> Must smite the chords rudely and hard,
> As with hammer or with mace;
> That they may render back
> Artful thunder, which conveys
> Secrets of the solar track.

These lines might have been written about Emily Dickinson, for she perfectly exemplifies the poet with special insights who is interested in content, not finished phrasing. For her, originally, poetry must have served as an anodyne for personal feelings, but it soon became the essence of her life. She hardly formulated an explicit poetic theory like Emerson or Poe, but from the comments scattered throughout her letters and poems her views on the obligations of a poet and the nature of poetry can be determined.

One of her poems, "Tell all the Truth but tell it slant," aptly describes her approach. The emphasis is on truth, on furnishing a complete account of life's experiences to illuminate hidden areas of knowledge and beauty. Since man's understanding is finite, this can be done only by indirection, by the poetic "slant," which sifts undifferentiated facts to uncover imaginatively truth's gold nuggets. Like Emerson and Poe she felt that the poet was a specially endowed seer who sought to discover "circumference" or the ultimate mysteries. Realistically she saw that such vision was necessarily limited, since "Nature is a Haunted House—but Art—a House that tries to be haunted." Of course, in dealing with truth the poet considered beauty, too, for the two were interchangeable aspects of the Divine nature. However, she never identified nature with the Divine, but contemplated the external world to understand better man's inner soul. She retained the romantic belief that inspiration and emotional response played an essential role in the poetic experience. "If I read a book," she said, "[and] it makes my whole body so cold no fire ever can warm me I know *that* is poetry. If I feel physically as if the top of my head were taken off, I know *that* is poetry. These are the only way I know it. Is there any other way?" Her imaginative and emotional nature delighted more in metaphorical effects and brilliant phrases than in the total organization of a poem.

From her own experience she knew the difficulties of the creative act, and in one remarkable poem, "Essential Oils—are wrung," compared the poetic process to the extraction of perfume from rose buds. The essence of an experience, the universal insight that the poet tries to express, is not obtained merely by being attuned to nature's processes or by slow organic growth; rather, poetic creation is a difficult task, depending more on the artist than on inspiration. As she imaginatively phrased it, only an unbearable stress could extract the precious essence. The second stanza broadens this concept and affirms the triumph of the artist whose fragrant creation will far outlast the corruptible rose and even the mortal artist.

She was fascinated by words and her best poems demonstrate a special awareness of root meanings and employ subtle connotations to deepen implication and association. Her real perplexities in selecting the exact word are attested by the endless variants her work sheets offered for words and phrases. For one phrase that was finally edited as "In eddies of the sun," she listed the following alternate choices:

> In fathoms in the sun
> In rapids of the sun
> In gambols with the sun
> In frenzies with the sun
> For frenzy of the sun
> In antics in the sun

Often this fascination with word patterns ends in a failure to perform the final ordering act of creation. Yet, as Charles Anderson has noted in his *Emily Dickinson's Poetry: Stairway of Surprise,* she rejuvenated the trite and hackneyed by various semantic and artistic devices:

Substitution of simple concrete terms for the abstract ones actually intended was her strategy for achieving vivid immediacy, and the

47

opposite for giving transcendent value to the homely. Juxtaposition of words out of different connotative spheres she employed for ironic contrast, as with the legal and amorous, and abrupt changes from one level of discourse to another for rhetorical shock, as from the serious to the comic, from eloquence to bald statement.

Reared within a heritage of economy and frugality, she ruthlessly cut through syntax and grammar to achieve conciseness. She omitted verbs, skipped conjunctions and prepositions, used dashes instead of conventional punctuation, and employed local pronunciation and dialect phrases to capture the "Attar" of her thoughts. "Capacity to Terminate," she called "A Specific Grace," and like the farmer wresting crops from a begrudging soil she cultivated this virtue. If at times her economy caused the poems to read like shorthand notations, it also gave them an exciting vibrancy.

Critics have traced endless influences and analogues for her poems in the Bible, Shakespeare, Blake, Emerson, and others, but she rarely imitated and was seldom derivative. She was not boasting to Higginson when she wrote that she "never consciously touch[ed] a paint, mixed by another person." Her vivid imagery and pithy expression drew on personal experiences rather than on classical or literary traditions. Certainly she used the Bible and Shakespeare and other writers for allusions, and she often composed improvisations upon familiar biblical stories. Her vitalization of orthodox religious terms like "election," "ecstasy," "grace," and "justification" constituted one of her most original achievements. Her love for precise definition (seen in numerous poems with lines beginning with "Faith is," "Love is"), her technical vocabulary, which drew widely from fields of medicine, mathematics, and grammar (words like "cauterize," "ratio," "ablative"), and her legal imagery (concentrating on words like "alibi," "enact," "surrogate") gave a pungency and terseness to her verses. Of course, nature furnished a ready source for imagery, though she constantly utilized eccentric subjects like the bat or worm to portray her sense of awe about natural processes and her dissatisfaction with the usual romantic treatment.

Also, her own world of household activities and local town events gave her poetry a piquancy and Amherst twang. Her colloquial expressions ("I wish I were a hay"), fondness for local spelling ("boquet," "Febuary"), unique use of the subjunctive voice to create a continuing present tense ("Eclipses be predicated"), and grammatical lapses ("at you and I," "It is Him") have continually outraged meticulous critics and delighted ordinary readers. Few poets could capture the laconic, yet involved, attitude with which a small town observed a funeral as she did in "There's been a Death, in the Opposite House." An idiomatic tone and a few selected details—windows opening "like a pod" and mattresses being flung out—rework familiar household activities to illustrate the terrible separation of death.

Emily Dickinson had a particular fondness for images dealing with sewing, clothing, housekeeping, the kitchen, and the garden. Often these were adroitly presented, as in her satire of pretentious town women in "What Soft—Cherubic Creatures—/ These Gentlewomen are." The central image compares these women to "plush" and "dimity" cloth, using the exact associations of a soft yielding material and a thin, overfine texture to characterize their weak natures and brittle attitudes. Also, she attached special symbolic significance to jewels and royal images, associating them with an elevation to a new aristocratic or "queen" state. A favorite Dickinson device was to contrast a familiar object with something momentous or awe-inspiring in order to shock the reader into a new appreciation or to sound ironic overtones. For example, the simple catalogue of daily actions in "I tie my Hat—I crease my Shawl" is most effective. Here the careful attention paid to meaningless gestures like arranging flowers or creasing a shawl illustrates poignantly how pain can enervate emotional responses.

Since Emily Dickinson was published posthumously and her manuscripts remained the personal notes of an unknown writer, certain stylistic traits that printing would have regularized were retained. She constantly capitalized nouns, adjectives, verbs, and even adverbs, as if trying to emphasize these words or to give them new dignity. Yet it is hard to decide in the holographs just when a letter is capitalized or not. Even where the capitalization seems fairly clear, it cannot be shown that the device creates special values. Rarely does it function organically to give new significance to outworn conventions, as in E. E. Cummings' consistent use of capitalization for important words. More likely the device simply reflects her tendency to overstate.

Far more perplexing is her use of dashes, for this device is intimately connected with meaning, musical effects, and over-all tone. This eccentricity often defeats the meaning, for it is difficult to determine when the dashes indicate a metrical pause or when they are to be treated as commas, semicolons, or periods. Again in the holographs the length and slant of the dashes vary so much that a final interpretation is impossible.[1] Certainly in some poems the dashes effectively highlight key phrases and provide a musical notation for reading the verse. Undoubtedly these stylistic devices were meaningful to her and were, perhaps, a definite experiment to loosen the stiff formality of conventional forms. But no matter how the poems are regularized, the final form will be somewhat arbitrary and selective. For example, consider these following two stanzas:

> Some—Work for Immortality—
> The Chiefer part, for Time—
> He—Compensates—immediately—
> The former—Checks—on Fame—
>
> Slow Gold—but Everlasting—
> The Bullion of Today—
> Contrasted with the Currency
> Of Immortality—

The complete poem states that a few select people create for immortality rather than for contemporary fame or immediate success. Throughout, the image of money, the changing currency of time versus the everlasting gold of immortality, emphasizes this idea. Most of the nouns, adjectives, and verbs are capitalized, but no real value system can be discerned. The "Some" working for immortality are appropriately capitalized, but so are the time servers ("Chiefer part"), while "former" referring to immortality is left uncapitalized. The capitalization of all the verbs, even the unimportant ones, cannot be explained. The dashes raise even more problems. The pause after "Some" gives effective emphasis, and the one at the end of the line serves as a semicolon or a conjunction. The dash after "Time" is presumably a full stop, while "He" is singled out to break the regular iambic pattern. But it is not clear why the adverb "immediately" is separated from its verb. Perhaps this gives the whole line a definite verse reading. The same approach is repeated

---

[1] An article by Edith Stamm, "Emily Dickinson: Poetry and Punctuation," furnishes a possible solution to this difficulty. Noting that Emily Dickinson's dashes seem to fall into three categories—horizontal (—), angular slant (/), and a reverse slant (\)—Professor Stamm relates these "irregular" marks to standard rhetorical practice in the middle nineteenth century. Most rhetoric books of this time used marks very similar to these for inflectional purposes, where (—) indicated a monotone, (/) a rising inflection, and (\) a falling accent. Thus Emily Dickinson placed these inflections after the words she wanted emphasized to indicate a proper reading for them. This theory appears to be the most adequate solution advanced so far, but when the holographs are read in the light of this system, it is frequently impossible to determine when a dash is horizontal, angular, or just a comma.

in the next line, but with jarring effects, as the disjointed phrases read awkwardly. If one considers the rhythm of the lines, then the dashes can function as caesuras, contributing to the metric pattern.

Other stylistic traits of Emily Dickinson are seen in this poem. None of the rhymes, neither "Time-Fame" nor "Today-Immortality," are exact. The alternating iambic pattern of six and seven syllables a line is broken twice in the first stanza. Emily Dickinson was not consciously trying to be metrically daring or shocking in her rhyming devices, as were Whitman in his bold experiments with verse and Lanier in his scientific study of sound patterns; rather, she explored older established forms to find a suitable medium for her thoughts. She loosened traditional set meters to capture the easy cadence of conversation and prose, but never attempted vers libre nor abandoned rhyming devices. The basic forms used in most of her verses were familiar to her from childhood. Watts's *Christian Psalmody,* which was in her father's library, became her verse primer. Its standard hymnal or ballad meter, four iambic lines, alternating three and four stresses a line with the second and fourth lines rhymed, was her favorite pattern. To avoid monotony she worked endless variations on this basic form, using eight-line stanzas, employing trochaic and other meters to vary the iambic, and letting the metric beat contrast with the meaning stress. Her great prosodic achievement was to enliven the droning monotony of the conventional hymn meter to a degree that its wooden practitioners would have thought impossible.

Her use of rhyme, which seemed so lawless and slovenly to formal critics like Higginson, was actually a liberation of conventional rhyming devices. She abandoned the stiff limitations of exact rhyme, where the final sound and accent were precisely repeated, returning to the much older poetic practice of approximate rhyme: identical and vowel rhyme (as in "move-remove," "see-buy"), imperfect rhyme (same vowel sounds followed by different consonants, as in "thing-in," "us-dust"), and suspended rhyme (different vowel sounds followed by the same consonant sounds, for example, "star-door," "reach-touch"). These rhymes were selected at will, and she freely varied the pattern within a single poem or stanza. Besides adding a great suppleness to her poetry, these approximate rhymes often capture the jarring discords and painful doubts expressed by the thought. However, this balance of content and form is not always so harmonious. Often the unusual rhymes seem unnecessary; the meter frequently becomes monotonous, while the subject matter remains too intense.

A poem on the importance of the human consciousness in not only perceiving but also creating truths exemplifies her usual metrical and rhyming practices. The poem has a regular common meter, alternating four and three stress iambic lines:

> Heaven is so far of the Mind
> That were the Mind dissolved—
> The Site—of it—by Architect
> Could not again be proved—
>
> 'Tis vast—as our Capacity
> As fair—as our idea—
>
> . . . .
> No further 'tis, than Here—

Still the mainly trochaic beat of the first line loosens the iambic pattern. Three of the first four lines end with a similar "d" sound, while "dissolved-proved" is an imperfect rhyme. In the second stanza New England dialect pronunciation makes "idea-here" almost a normal vowel rhyme. The balanced meter reinforces the tone of contemplation, while the approximate rhymes and trochaic inversions break the uniform pattern to reflect the unexpectedness of the thought.

The full extent of Emily Dickinson's achievement can be illustrated by an analysis of "Because I could not stop for Death." The poem deals with her favorite subject, the effect of death upon a human being. Instead of the human fear or religious awe usually associated with death, it is portrayed as a restful trip, a pleasant journey with a courteous visitor and an unnoticed third traveler, immortality. Yet one senses undercurrents of terror and shock, especially in the last three stanzas, as the passenger gradually becomes aware of the utter finality of the trip. The tensions inherent in this ambivalent approach to death depend heavily on the domestic imagery and the casual tone. One is startled to hear awesome death addressed as a kindly gentleman whose gracious manner soothes the victim and whose invitation is gladly accepted as from an old family friend or lover. In fact the erotic undertones, barely hinted at in this opening and later intensified by the bridal gown imagery, explore another facet in death's complex personality. The literal description of death contains no real terror, for a tone of easy familiarity and old world charm continues throughout the poem.

The first stanza describes the narrator as so engrossed in household activities that she cannot spare time for death's call:

> Because I could not stop for Death—
> He kindly stopped for me—

> The Carriage held but just Ourselves—
> And Immortality.

Only his kindness and consideration compel her to steal a few minutes for a short ride. Her reluctance hides the harsh reality that she has no choice, that her carriage is a hearse, and that the lover's outing is a somber journey to the grave. Even immortality's presence, openly hinting at the soul's departure from the body and the longer pilgrimage into eternity, is barely acknowledged and quickly forgotten. This idea of a casual trip is expanded in the second stanza with the key phrase "my labor and my leisure." For death actually heightens one's perception of time. The precious, fleeting qualities of life, its mixture of work and joy, are now freshly appreciated. One regrets the loss of pleasures, while being glad to forfeit life's terrible pressures and fears.

With the reiteration of "passed" in the third stanza and the increasing awareness of time, the slow journey begins to hasten:

> We passed the School, where Children strove
> At Recess—in the Ring—
> We passed the Fields of Gazing Grain—
> We passed the Setting Sun—

As the corpse is physically carried through the town to the outlying fields, the soul finally crosses through the barriers of temporal time and the mind reviews its past life: childhood, schooling, the ripeness of maturity, and finally the darkening red of evening age. Significantly even the children's world is a mixture of play ("Recess") and tensions ("strove"), enclosed by the ring of society's rules and customs. The physical and spiritual implications of "we passed" are intensified by the "Gazing Grain" image, which both mocks and parallels the inert corpse. The rich grain gazes indifferently, almost hostilely. There can be no such equivalent death in nature, only a laying fallow after the harvest, followed by an eventual spring rebirth. Yet nature's eternal hope echoes the presence and purpose of the other passenger, immortality. The final image, a traditional comparison of a sunset's declining warmth and brightness to old age, prepares for the final stage of the journey.

Stanza four marks a definite transition from the accelerating tone of the country outing:

> Or rather—He passed Us—
> The Dews drew quivering and chill—
> For only Gossamer, my Gown—
> My Tippet—only Tulle—

Even the metrical shift from a four- to a three-stress line technically indicates a new mood. The poet corrects her earlier statement about passing the sun, for nature controls, not man. With increasing darkness comes a dampness and chill, heightened by the heavy alliteration and sharp "i" sounds. Now the poet is frighteningly aware of how inadequate her preparations for the journey have been. The sheer wedding gown offers no protection from the cold, and it indicates how completely her sophisticated caller has deceived her with his assurances of a warm and friendly trip. Still, death has further surprises for his alarmed companion. Her bridal chamber is a horrifying combination of an actual mansion and the swelling mound of a graveyard tomb.

> We paused before a House that seemed
> A Swelling of the Ground—
> The Roof was scarcely visible—
> The Cornice—in the Ground—
>
> Since then—'tis Centuries—and yet
> Feels shorter than the Day
> I first surmised the Horses' Heads
> Were toward Eternity—

Here the terror is achieved without any morbid description of moldering bones and worms so frequently used by Poe. The tenuous bond between life and death is "scarcely visible" as the poet finally perceives her destination. Just as the reader prepares for a gruesome entry into the tomb, the perspective changes. With the end of the journey death departs and the poet reviews the trip from the vantage point of eternity. The sudden change from present reality to the new dimension of limitless time shows how completely death severs all connections with life. This surprising shift jars the reader after the beguiling leisureliness of the journey, while the final image of the horses' heads turned toward eternity magnificently conveys the awesome power and impervious majesty of death. The dramatic emphasis placed upon the word "Eternity" highlights the separation between man's limited earthly existence and the expanse of infinity. Paradoxically the word not only conveys the chill finality of death but also indicates that the soul has now ascended into a new state of existence. In fact, "Eternity" hints at the possibility of religious immortality, which was faintly suggested in stanza one.

The poem masterfully handles the effect of death's unexpected visit upon the victim, viewing her progression from flustered self-pleasure and comfortable anticipation to gradual fear and doubt into a full realization of death's deception and terrifying purpose. Throughout, death is seen from various perspectives: as a welcome relief from life's tensions; as a force which heightens one's satisfaction with life; as a lover gently conveying one to hidden pleasures; as a cynical caller who poses beneath a cordial exterior; and finally as a solemn guide leading one to the threshold of immortality. In this poem Emily Dickinson's profound views of death and immortality are rendered with an artistic perfection that very few lyrics surpass.

5

NATURE

O NE OF Emily Dickinson's nature poems, "What mystery pervades a wall," examines the mystery and awe often associated
with a deep well. Bypassing the well's familiar home use, the author
notes that one rarely penetrates beyond its surface reflection and that
further probing only displays an opaque depth. After contrasting
her hesitancy and fear when approaching a well with nature's easy
intimacy, she concludes that nature remains mysterious, for the
more deeply we scrutinize her processes, the more complex and bewildering they become. Essentially nature exists as an alien, baffling force that defies full comprehension. Emily Dickinson taunts
those who laud nature the most, the gushing romantics, the scien-
tists, and the visionary pantheists, for their assumed familiarity be-
trays a lack of perception. Regretfully she acknowledges that even
those closest to nature, the poets and thinkers, also fail.

Certainly she felt that nature somehow participated in the mystery
of divinity, but she never believed that the natural order paralleled
the Divine or that intense study would develop mystic knowledge.
She rarely expressed the inherent pantheism found in the transcendental oversoul, and only in a poem like "All Circumstances
are the Frame" is God tentatively identified with nature. As Mordecai Marcus in his unpublished dissertation has demonstrated,
many early poems found a hope for immortality in the seasonal
movement from winter to spring. Many of her conventional nature
poems praised nature as "the Gentlest Mother," who soothed and
comforted her bruised children. She delighted in nature's external
pageantry and effused sentimentally about the red breast of the
robin and the butterfly's beautiful colors. Yet, her later poems
showed a distrust of such analogies, ironically contrasting nature's
ordered majesty with man's doomed mortality. Nature mocked
rather than comforted man. Usually her better poems stressed nature's decaying and corruptive power. Death lay at the core of

56

nature, continually threatening man with extinction. Many poems like "The Morning after Wo" and "I dreaded that first Robin, so" analyze nature's betrayal of those hearts that loved her best. In a poem about the frost's beheading a flower, "Apparently with no surprise," she even questioned if nature had any meaning at all, for a universe that proceeds indifferently and is untouched by such crimes haunts one with terror.

The destructive power of nature's winds, rains, and lightning storms also impressed her. Still, her principal response to nature was a fascination with its continual change, the daily passage of the sun, the sudden alterations wrought by storms, the miracle of spring growth, and the deceptive appearance of Indian summer. She was intrigued by the illusory, fleeting essence of nature and awed by its connection with the divine process. The unusual and the odd areas of nature attracted her, and she transmuted unpoetic subjects like crickets, flies, weeds, and rats into art. Though acutely observant and aware of precise detail, she distrusted scientific analysis and scoffed at its attempts to codify all nature. She tempered her genuine enthusiasm for the beauty of external nature with an awareness of its innate mystery and strangeness. Never certain of any clear correspondence among God, nature, and man, she remained a skeptic who both admired and doubted.

Emily Dickinson's refusal to employ nature as a guide for moral behavior and her unusual skill in presenting vivid sense impressions highlight the differences between her and other writers of nature poetry in nineteenth-century America. Her poems on birds, flowers, insects, and natural processes rarely become didactic or insist upon divine analogues, as Bryant does in "To a Waterfowl" and Emerson in "The Rhodora." Often her nature poems are sentimental and her domestic conceits excessively developed and overly feminine. For example, the image of the sunset as a housewife cleaning the sky in "She sweeps with many-colored Brooms" is laboriously extended for twelve lines and offends artistic taste with its cloying metaphors about dusting the pond and plying spotted brooms. But she could etch genre portraits and achieve local color effects with the best regional artists, while her feeling for picturesque detail and whimsical tone raised scores of these sketches to the level of good poetry.

The drama of sunrise and sunset, particularly, attracted her. One poem, "I'll tell you how the Sun rose," uses a series of action verbs and domestic images to convey the quick surprise and changing color of the dawn. The diffusing rays of the sun unravel as decorative ribbons in a milliner's shop; the color is almost palpable and drowns the steeples in its surging amethyst; and the changing lights dart from tree to tree like squirrels. Even the final image of the hills untying their bonnets, which veers slightly toward the sentimental, exactly reproduces the fuzziness and haze that the glow of the rising sun causes behind the hills. The remainder of the poem falters as the sunset is described as a priest gently leading his flock home. A better poem on the same subject opens with this arresting conceit:

> Blazing in Gold and quenching in Purple
> Leaping like Leopards to the Sky
> Then at the feet of the old Horizon
> Laying her spotted Face to die

The wondrous interplay of motion, color, and heat captured in these lines is intensified by the spectacular image of the leopard. His spotted yellow and brown body leaps out in an exuberant display of agility and majestic power to connote sensuously the grandeur of the sun's passage. The final image of the sun as the "Juggler of Day" relates nature's seeming defiance of the laws of gravity by suspending the sun in mid-air to the art of a juggler in deceiving his audience. Nature, for the poet, becomes the master illusionist, since it merely pretends motion for the benefit of earth-bound humans. Both these poems are characteristic of Emily Dickinson's gift for expansive, highly original images as well as of her tendency to neglect ordered structure.

Like the daily miracle of sunrise and sunset, the dramatic occurrences of summer rains and lightning storms impressed her. The unleashed power of these storms, with their complete dominion over man's world, occasioned a sense of "circumference" and religious fear which deepened their picturesque effects. "The Wind begun to knead the Grass" employs touches of local color, which, together with a fantastic array of action verbs, exhibit the mysterious chaos of a sudden summer downpour:

> The Wagons quickened on the Street—
> The Thunders gossiped low—
> The Lightning showed a Yellow Head—
> And then a livid Toe—

As the waters "wreck" the sky and lightning "quarters" a tree, the poet observes half-reverently and half-humorously that somehow the storm "overlooked my Father's house." A later storm poem, "There came a Wind like a Bugle," enlarges the feeling of reverence and surprise that any life survives such onslaughts. Synesthetic phrases like "Green Chill," "Emerald Ghost," "Doom's electric Moccasin," vividly designate the tension-filled pause before the storm breaks. As Charles Anderson notes in his illuminating discussion of this and the other two storm poems, reality here has become "fluid and illusory, on the point of disappearing." Even the violent shaking of the steeple bells seems to herald a final judgment. One other storm poem, "It sounded as if the Streets were running," condenses a similar situation into eight lines to emphasize the circumference of the moment. With a familiar Dickinson twist, reality returns as the awed citizens creep from their barricades to view nature.

Emily Dickinson loved flowers and had a greater knowledge of them than any other item in nature, but her poems on the rose, the buttercup, and the daisy were usually conventional and sentimental. Only a poem on the arbutus has the freshness and precise detail that so distinguish her best work:

> Pink—small—and punctual—
> Aromatic—low
> Covert—in April—
> Candid—in May—

These clipped, humorous adjectives focus on the furtive beauty of this early spring arrival. Again the rest of the poem pales into clichés like "Dear to the Moss" and "Bold little Beauty." Still a comparison of this poem with Whittier's "The Trailing Arbutus" highlights the differences between Emily Dickinson and the writers of the genteel tradition. Unlike her detached, precise notations, Whittier's poem merely describes the arbutus as "The trailing spring flower tinted like a shell." He concentrates on the surrounding bleak atmosphere of receding snows and dead branches to enhance the moral that even in the most "lowly, clogged, and pent" lives beauty and goodness can survive.

Bees, birds, and insects seemed to free her imagination, as she wrote some of her best genre poems about them. She was particularly fond of bees and delighted in caricaturing their incessant activity.

> Bees are Black, with Gilt Surcingles—
> Buccaneers of Buzz.
> Ride abroad in ostentation
> And subsist on Fuzz.

Emily Dickinson's whimsey and burlesque skill are brilliantly demonstrated here. The humorous rhymes parody the bees' attempts to be intrepid, glamorous buccaneers, while their imitative religious attire ("Gilt Surcingles"), their weak monotonous buzz, and their fragile diet of fuzz contribute to the comic mood. The second stanza discusses their fuzz sustenance and place in the universe on a mock metaphysical plane. A scholastic distinction, "Fuzz ordained—not Fuzz contingent," states that their food is essential, rather than accidental, being close to the core of life ("Marrows of the hill"). The heavy philosophic terms and concluding hint of universal destruction spoof the bees' showy, self-satisfied lives. Another light poem, "A Bee his burnished Carriage," describes the honey gathering process as the frank seduction of a quivering rose.

Two of Emily Dickinson's descriptions of birds, the oriole in "One of the ones that Midas touched," and the blue jay in "No Brigadier throughout the Year," dazzle with their exuberant images and extravagant conceits. Her most famous nature portrait is that of the hummingbird:

> A Route of Evanescence
> With a revolving Wheel—
> A Resonance of Emerald—
> A Rush of Cochineal—
> And every Blossom on the Bush
> Adjusts its tumbled Head—
> The mail from Tunis, probably,
> . . . .

Besides remaining a vivid poetic response to nature, it also conveys her sense of nature's mystery and elusiveness. The poem reworks the hackneyed image of the ruby-throated hummingbird to present the sensation of its whirling flight and disappearance before our startled eyes. The images focus upon the bird's vanishing characteristics and its great speed to present a synesthetic blur of color and motion like the simultaneous action exposures of present-day photography. The heavy alliteration, the repetitive rhetorical pattern, and the daring association of its red and green color with sound vibrations evoke the illusion of evanescence. The second section dramatizes this disappearance by its sudden shift to the bird's bewildering effects upon the flowers. The surprised blossoms, still trembling from the bird's passage, humorously comment that the visit was probably just the morning's mail from Tunis. Even this glancing reference to Shakespeare's *The Tempest*, a play filled with magic illusion and vanishing spirits, adds to the pageantry of the hummingbird's evanescence.

In her best nature poems Emily Dickinson skillfully deepens her concrete detail and sensuous surface imagery by contrasting the world of man with that of nature. For example, "A Bird came down the Walk" can be read literally as an exact description of the quick, furtive movements of a bird as it eats, hops about a garden, and then flies gracefully away. The surface tone is humorous and wryly ironic, for she laughs at the bird's fear of a beetle and his distrust of the crumb she offers. By the final stanza the tone is one of awe and aesthetic response to the bird's beautiful flight. Yet various undercurrents of fear demand that we read deeper into the poem, for the bird's initial casualness changes into hesitancy and suspicion. Even the description of the bird eating the worm occasions uneasy humor. The first two stanzas are the most concrete:

> A Bird came down the Walk—
> He did not know I saw—
> He bit an Angleworm in halves
> And ate the fellow, raw,
>
> And then he drank a Dew
> From a convenient Grass—
> And then hopped sidewise to the Wall
> To let a Beetle pass—

The stanza's quick trimeter lines, varied by one tetrameter, are reined by a regular iambic beat and exact rhyme. At his first appearance the bird is humorously pictured on a casual afternoon stroll. His eating the worm is a natural act, but the precise description of the bite and the rhyme emphasis given to "raw" stress the unpleasant aspects of the meal, jolting the accustomed picture of a bird's harmlessness. The next stanza whimsically continues the meal with the play on the word "grass" and the incongruity of drinking a dew. The sudden appearance of the beetle subtly shifts the tone as the bird's surface courtesy conceals the underlying struggle among nature's creatures.

The slight changes in meter, the use of run-on lines, and the approximate rhymes in stanzas three and four break the exact pattern of the opening and intensify the mood of fear and danger. The bird's eyes are rapid and hurried, like "frightened Beads" rolling wildly in a glass. As the bird stirs his velvet head, the poet reveals herself and offers a crumb. The irony in attempting to placate the bird's fears is evident, since nature has already supplied sufficient food for the bird. The capitalization of "crumb" and its end-rhyme position further accentuate the lack of understanding between man

and nature. The final lines in the poem fully present this separation
by describing the bird's serene flight:

> And he unrolled his feathers
> And rowed him softer home—
>
> Than Oars divide the Ocean,
> Too silver for a seam—
> Or Butterflies, off Banks of Noon
> Leap, plashless as they swim.

The assonance of "o" and "a," the blending of "p" and "l" sounds,
and the conceit of the sky-sea and bird-boat develop the feeling of
eternal serenity. In particular the final lines portray a world of
aesthetic perfection, where fragile, varicolored butterflies leap gracefully off the sun's hot sands into the liquid coolness of the sky.

Drawing the poem's various strands together, one sees how skillfully Emily Dickinson has moved beyond mere physical description.
Basically the poem considers the ambivalence of nature's beauty and
grace having such a destructive core. Beneath its tranquil surface
exists a world of fear and continual warfare. Yet, nature effortlessly
combines these disparate traits as the bird, which ferociously eats
the worm, also achieves aesthetic immortality in its flight. Man's
spying and his useless offer of a crumb lead to the bird's final rejection and illuminate another theme: nature's superior self-sufficiency over man's fumbling awkwardness.

One of Emily Dickinson's most distinctive nature groupings deals
with the neglected and grotesque aspects of nature—the rat, mushroom, fly, bat, snake, weeds, frog, stones, spider, and caterpillar.
Although romantic writers shunned these aspects of nature and
earnest moralists ignored their existence, Emily Dickinson revitalized
the old clichés about nature. In our own time poets often juxtapose
"garlic and sapphires in the mud," mingling the ugly with the beautiful, but in the late nineteenth century such writing was not popular. The lighter, humorous side of nature's offshoots is depicted in
"The Mushroom is the Elf of Plants." Drawing upon the fairy associations clustered about elves, she whimsically explores the illusory, transitory qualities that underlie nature's surface. The fantastic
comparisons and mock heroic phrasing like "Vegetation's Juggler,"
"Germ of Alibi," and "surreptitious scion" capture the eccentric,
defiant character of the mushroom. The poem concludes with nature's helpless chagrin over this rebel, whose unaccountable life is
epitomized by a term of religious deviation and ungrammatical
phrasing:

> Had Nature an Apostate—
> That Mushroom—it is Him!

In "The Rat is the conciset Tenant" another odd creature mocks man's complacent trust in law and social patterns. As if baiting conventional romantic writers, Emily Dickinson wins our approval and admiration for this repulsive rodent. Throughout, the satire is double-edged; she feigns puzzlement over the rat's parasitical traits, while ridiculing the chain-of-being concept and man's social laws.

> The Rat is the conciset Tenant.
> He pays no Rent.
> Repudiates the Obligation—
> On Schemes intent

The brief declarative phrases fit the rat's exact nature, which casually ignores all that is unessential to his own ends. Not only does he fail to pay for food and lodging but he completely denies any moral responsibility. His "schemes" balk human intelligence, since man cannot ignore such amoral acts; and they annoy human superiority, since man's hate cannot move him. Throughout the poem the over-use of legal terms and mixture of exact and approximate rhyme mock man's efforts to "decree" proper social responsibility for the rat. The poem concludes that the rat is "Lawful as Equilibrium." He lives outside ordinary restrictions and poses to us the frustrating cleavage between man and nature.

A far more disturbing investigation of nature's famous mystery occurs in "A narrow Fellow in the Grass." Here Emily Dickinson examines the terror and awe that a snake's presence can occasion. A series of artistic progressions develop the snake image into a symbol of the unknown. At first the snake is treated playfully; his sudden "notice" and quick movements fascinate the viewer and even convey a sense of regality and power as his coiling body is likened to a "Whip lash/ Unbraiding in the Sun." Still, disturbing undertones are sounded by the adjective "narrow" and the snake's hidden, gliding motion. His fondness for primitive swamps, where no corn ever grows, hints at the snake's biblical associations with evil and the desolate places of the earth. The concluding stanzas contrast the barefoot poet and her love for the rest of nature with the dread that this creature inspires:

> But never met this Fellow
> Attended, or alone
> Without a tighter breathing
> And Zero at the Bone—

The final image connotes the absolute terror that the snake brings. A blank negation, like Melville's chilling description of the whiteness of the whale, paralyzes man's spirit and pushes him closer to a frightening vacuum. From an interested, mildly amused treatment of his external characteristics, the poem develops the snake's association with man's fear of the unknown and evil itself. Here the sense of hidden terror behind nature's surface beauty fascinates and frightens the onlooker.

Another poem, dealing with the bat, is perhaps her finest treatment of nature's misfits. Though the poem never achieves the frightening intensity of the verses about the snake, it raises some perplexing questions concerning the purpose behind creation and man's limitations in comprehending the divine plan. The early stanzas imaginatively catalogue the bat's form, color, and activities, stressing his grotesque qualities. The heavy alliteration, Latinate phrasing, and cryptic shifts from line to line heighten this strangeness and lead into a puzzled discussion of God's reasons for creating the bat. One possible theme is, of course, the inability of man's finite mind to discern just what God has planned for all aspects of creation. The bat appears useless and eccentric to us, but just as we are unable to hear his song, perhaps we cannot understand how "beneficent" he is within the total order of the universe. However, as we continue to examine the poem, certain ironies of phrase and an overall questioning tone indicate a less orthodox position.

> The Bat is dun, with wrinkled Wings—
> Like fallow Article—
> And not a song pervade his Lips—
> Or none perceptible.
>
> His small Umbrella quaintly halved
> Describing in the Air
> An Arc alike inscrutable
> Elate Philosopher.

The first two stanzas center on the repulsive aspects of the bat. His depressing grayish-brown color and his unattractive wings present him as an outcast among the beauties of nature. A weird combination of mouse and bird traits, he is a curious, unfinished creature ("fallow Article"). Here "fallow" also indicates his seeming uselessness, while "Article" conveys his divided and dependent nature. Her perplexity about no perceptible sounds has only been clarified by modern research. These investigations have shown that the bat orients himself by ultrasonic cries that are of too high a frequency for human ears to hear and thus he avoids obstacles in the dark. In Emily Dickinson's time the bat's ability to fly in the dark remained a mystery, separating the bat from ordinary creatures.[1] The umbrella image, besides depicting the bat's thin wing structure, connotes his nervous, hesitant personality, which always needs protection. Of course, his flight ("Arc") is mysterious and unexplainable, since he is guided by sound vibrations. How the bat embodies wisdom which lifts our spirits ("Elate Philosopher") is uncertain, unless one connects his inscrutable flight with the mystery of nature. Perhaps the phrase is best understood as an ironic hit at poet-philosophers like Whitman who found divinity in a blade of grass.

The next stanza overburdens the unimportant bat with heavy philosophical terms to re-enforce this ironic tone. One finds comic rather than cosmic significance in the bat's life. In bombastic fashion the poet employs biblical phrases and rhetorical patterns to topple all attempts at grandeur and seriousness. The expected praise of God's goodness in creating an ordered universe is reversed as the poet merely notes that God has withheld the full extent of the evil traditionally associated with the bat.

> To his adroit Creator
> Ascribe no less the praise—
> Beneficent, believe me,
> His Eccentricities—

The last stanza seems to resolve these doubts, but the previous analysis of this misfit belies the adroitness of the creator. Instead, one suspects that God himself has little control over his "bat" creation. The poet almost parodies the orthodox approach to creation by insisting that the bat is beneficent even though he cannot be understood. This term "beneficent" aptly captures the poem's ambivalent approach. Certainly many bats beneficially eat insects and pollinate plants, yet the fruit bat and vampire bat spread disease and even kill. Finally, the overstated "believe me" echoes hollowly like the parrot chant of an uncomprehending schoolboy and jars any pious acceptance. Instead of serene confidence in God's divine plan, the poem ends with this ambiguity. On the whole, the poem once again demonstrates Emily Dickinson's delight in exploring the religious basis of the unusual and the odd.

Though the daily movement of the sun, the power of storms, and

[1] For this information concerning the bat I am indebted to Professor Robert J. Toft of the Biology Department of Cornell College, Iowa. Also many of the ideas for my analysis of the cricket in "Further in Summer than the Birds" were furnished by Professor Toft.

the strangeness of creation impressed her, the larger seasonal cycles and the fleeting aspects of material beauty drew her most imaginative response. The miracle of the barren winter containing the seeds of fruitful summer and the rich crops foretelling the death of harvest never ceased to fascinate her. Realizing that no one could fully understand nature's processes, she restrained her enthusiastic response to the change of seasons with undertones of this mystery. If the essence of nature defied explanation, at least poetic insight furnished perceptive readers with some outline of its "haunted house." This challenge of describing nature's elusiveness occasioned some of her most speculative poems.

Of course, spring was a favored season, since it displayed the wonder of rebirth and openly promised the warm beauty of summer. She called spring a time sent directly from God and particularly welcomed March as the herald of spring. From light local color sketches like "An altered look about the hills" she moved to more thoughtful considerations of the whole cycle in "New feet within my garden go." The opening stanza of this poem expresses the poet's wonder at the first stirrings of plant life and the initial song of a bird. In the second stanza her pleasure diminishes as she contrasts the new children playing upon the green with the new dead sleeping in graves. Finally her joyous response to spring is muted by the knowledge that it is only a part of a complete cycle that punctually arrives and leads again to winter. Since the inexorable seasonal change forbids permanent growth or lasting beauty, spring's hope deceives and brings pensiveness.

"A Light exists in Spring" is perhaps her best analysis of the peculiar awe that this season inspires. The poem deals with March, the pivot of the new year, when spring transforms the cold, barren winter. Spring's hope is compared to a rarely glimpsed light which carries regal and religious associations to signify the psychological insights that occur at such a moment. Coming as influx of grace, this illumination heightens man's emotional awareness of spring's mysteries and enlarges his poignant sense of estrangement. The "light" image of the first stanza, with its suggestions of purity and freshness, is enriched by these lines:

> A Color stands abroad
> On Solitary Fields
> That Science cannot overtake

Here the color, unlike the molten gold of summer or the mellow red of autumn, remains indefinite, standing regally aloof. The quality of this experience is neither rational nor pragmatic; even science fails to comprehend it. The middle stanzas examine the light's mystical aspect, which reaches "upon the furthest Slope" known to man, into the depths of the human soul. A military conceit changes this solemn tone by describing the light's disappearance with humorous precision. In the final stanza the poet states the significance of the experience, emphasizing its religious value and the desolation that follows its departure.

> A quality of loss
> Affecting our Content
> As Trade had suddenly encroached
> Upon a Sacrament.

The return of reality, harshly phrased as "Trade," typifies the proceedings of a large impersonal company interested only in measurable gain and unconcerned about religious intangibles. The moment's sacramental aspects, displaying God's grace and power, are now lost. Throughout the poem, motion and light images are constantly interwoven to suggest the longing and awe that the light brings. Thus the physical experience of an early spring day is transformed into a moment of religious illumination.

Though summer brought a full blossoming of her beloved plants and flowers, Emily Dickinson never successfully captured its special atmosphere. One of her earliest attempts, "The Gentian weaves her fringes," celebrates the death of summer with a mock heroic sermon, funeral procession, and burial service. Another impressionistic sketch, "It will be Summer—eventually," pictorially views the season from the vantage point of midwinter to hint at the underlying cyclical process. Her only memorable poem on summer characteristically deals with the sense of loss that summer's departure brings:

> As imperceptibly as Grief
> The Summer lapsed away—
> Too imperceptible at last
> To seem like Perfidy—

The word "imperceptible" guides the whole poem, and its solemn, dignified associations are repeated by "Perfidy," "Quietness distilled," and "Sequestered Afternoon." Summer's passage is described as a gentle escape that, though barely observed, still occasions grief. True grief appears all embracing and eternal, just as summer overwhelms our senses with its warm rich promise, but in time the demands of life absorb sorrow. The "l" and "p" blends modulate the tone and focus on the liquid sound of "lapsed" to convey the ebbing of summer's power. Summer's departure is not a sudden betrayal which brings outrage but is so "imperceptible" that the loss goes nearly unnoticed. The middle stanzas further define this loss as a "harrowing Grace," coming with afternoon's quiet and the approaching twilight. The feeling of estrangement deepens when nature is personified as a house guest who stays for a time, winning our love and devotion, but who refuses to remain. Though gracious, the guest's manner becomes increasingly aloof and disdainful. The slight change of "the summer" into "our summer" emphasizes the intimacy, while summer's fragile passage "without a Wing/ Or service of a Keel" conveys a sense of aesthetic satisfaction. In very few poems is the poignancy and ephemeral quality of the seasonal movement so finely presented.

Emily Dickinson once remarked: "These Indian-Summer Days with their peculiar Peace remind me of those stillest things that no one can disturb. . . . I suppose we are all thinking of Immortality, at times so stimulatedly that we cannot sleep. Secrets are interesting, but they are also solemn—and speculate with all our might, we cannot ascertain." No time of year ever evoked more imaginative responses nor seemed so allied to immortality. One of her earliest poems on the subject, "These are the days when Birds come back," illustrates how profoundly she probed nature's deceptive quality. The theme turns on the original meaning of Indian summer, whatever in the new world looked like the real thing, but was not. Musing on this, she considers the blinding illusion that surface beauty creates, the religious significance in this seasonal life-death cycle, the failure of the scientific approach, which so easily brands the season a "fraud," and finally the need for a child's trusting acceptance. The structure of the poem exemplifies this mixture of disbelief and faith. The first three stanzas develop her practical realization that the phenomenon is a "blue and gold mistake," while the last three celebrate her acceptance of the illusion as a symbol of fundamental natural laws. A very formal metric and rhetorical pattern, an interlocking rhyme scheme, and decorative religious imagery contribute to the dignified mood of the poem.

The early stanzas stress the deceptive quality of this imitation summer, which easily deceives man but deceives only a few of nature's perceptive creatures. Utilizing local superstitions about the bee's wisdom, she contrasts his sage refusal to believe with her desire that the "plausibility" be true. The middle stanzas contain the heart of the poem:

Till ranks of seeds their witness bear—
And softly thro' the altered air
Hurries a timid leaf.

Oh Sacrament of summer days,
Oh Last Communion in the Haze—
Permit a child to join.

The fourth stanza is the transitional link between the two attitudes presented in the poem. First she asserts her knowledge of the illusion after toying with acceptance in the third stanza. The seeds flying through the changed air are the final deposit before winter. They are a "witness" to the coming change and desolation that this false summer shields, for even the falling leaf echoes this motif of extinction. As George Arms notes in his explication of the poem, these seeds contain the potential life that must die and be buried before spring's resurrection can come again. The pun on "altered," which sounds like "altared," prepares for her qualified acceptance of this mystery. The following stanza affirms the religious value of the illusion by the image of Holy Communion. As the outward sign of an inward spiritual reality, the Eucharist wafer is a profound symbol for what is occurring in nature. These warm summer-like days are indicative of the seasonal cycle of change and death. What appears to be deception actually represents a basic religious law. The cycle of nature moves into the death of winter only to allow a rebirth in spring. The religious images sanction these Indian summer days as the last rites for a dying year and as a preparation for immortality. Though she abandons her detached position to partake of this truth, it comes in an ambiguous "Haze." In Charles Anderson's phrasing, "this desire for belief," in the final stanza, "becomes plaintive; with all the evidence against her the poet can only say, Permit me to become a child and partake, sacramentally, of immortality! The poem itself is a kind of 'last Communion' between her critical mind and yearning heart."

The winter season never had much appeal for Emily Dickinson, although she wrote two imaginative descriptions of a winter snowstorm, "It sifts from Leaden Sieves" and "Like Brooms of Steel." Only one of her better poems uses the framework of winter to explore the despair that the season often brings. Like the poem on spring's mystic illumination, "There's a certain Slant of light" focuses on the paradox of light. Instead of brightening and clarifying, these slanted winter rays oppress and afflict, threatening the soul's faith. Numerous religious associations deepen this despair and indicate the light's function as a testing ground for the soul. These despairing moments not only bring pain but are valuable imperial things that inspire awe and complete submission. Nature herself bows to this power, which is finally compared to death, since the light pushes man's faith to its farthest limits. The poem again illustrates man's inadequate control over nature and the desperation with which he fights for survival. Mordecai Marcus has further commented that man's inability to know an existence beyond death causes this despair, while man's psychological and emotional pain is paralleled by the underlying decay process in nature.

Emily Dickinson constantly examined man's relation to the world of natural phenomena. Eschewing easy religious affirmation and effusive romantic enthusiasm, she looked closely at natural objects, contemplated their function, then recorded her responses with scrupulous exactness. Once, when discussing a poem's movement from delight to wisdom, Robert Frost remarked that "like a piece of ice on a hot stove the poem must ride on its own melting." The following three poems on the grandeur of the northern lights, the simplicity of a stone, and the pensive song of crickets exemplify the slow artistic melting of material image into provocative thought.

"Of Bronze—and Blaze" considers a display of northern lights, which sometimes could be seen during the fall in Amherst. The poem treats one of the oldest poetic subjects—the insufficiency of man when compared to the infinite grandeur of God's creation. Numerous psalms like "The Heavens declare the glory of God; and the firmament sheweth his handywork" have similar themes, but Emily Dickinson concentrates on man's response to these splendors and adds wry touches of irony that are quite alien to these devotional songs. Like the psalms the poem moves from a brief description of natural phenomena and their attributes to their effect upon the observer below, as he vainly attempts to imitate their grandeur. The second section of the poem enlarges these philosophical considerations, contrasting man's temporary achievements and mortality with the vastness and glory of eternity.

> Of Bronze—and Blaze—
> The North—Tonight—
> So adequate—it forms—
> So preconcerted with itself—
> So distant—to alarms—
>
> . . . .

These opening lines dramatically emphasize both the color and form of the northern lights. "Bronze" designates the striking blend of red and gold seen against the black night, while "Blaze" connotes jagged, flaming peaks streaking across the sky. Even the set pauses between each poetic foot add to the solemnity of the scene. The north's grandeur is portrayed as a reflection of the Divine, being completely self-contained and implacable. Adjectives like "adequate" and "preconcerted" portray the Godhead gazing upon itself in perfect contentment, impervious in its splendid isolation to the insignificant concerns ("alarms") of the world below.

> Infects my simple spirit
> With Taints of Majesty—
> Till I take vaster attitudes—
> And strut upon my stem—
> Disdaining Men, and Oxygen,
> For Arrogance of them—

From the contemplation of God's majesty the poem shifts to the responses of the human observer. This brilliant display, with its regal "unconcern," infects her simple spirit. Just as a small scratch can infect the body with poison, so these distant lights can unduly excite man's aspirations. Though her finite soul can catch only "taints" of this splendor, mere streaks of washed-out color, she is filled with longing and so takes vaster attitudes and struts. The ironic undertones in the word "strut," the suggestion of the flower's minute size in "stem," and its ephemeral beauty indicate the hopelessness of man's attempts to assume divine attributes. The soul's eternal longings and pitiful efforts to impress are laughable, yet bring some nobility, since they are undertaken without hope of success. Her strutting imitation brings arrogant disdain for others who have not perceived the grandeur of these lights. It can even cause tragic pride, for under its influence man might try to exist without necessary oxygen and perish. Though this moment of ecstasy affords the soul a temporary mystic experience, the over-all mood is ironic, underlining the pathetic insufficiency of any attempts to copy the Divine.

The final section puts these endeavors into the perspective of mortality and eternity:

> My Splendors, are Menagerie—
> But their Completeless Show
> Will entertain the Centuries
> When I, am long ago,
> An Island in dishonored Grass—
> Whom none but Beetles—know.

Her splendors, the things achieved under the influence of these inspiring lights, are called "Menagerie," a mere collection of bizarre, wild animals in a tawdry side show mocked by nature's solemn dignity.[2] "Their" refers to the northern lights, which symbolize the enduring grandeur and beauty of God. This show, God's master exhibition, is no menagerie but "Completeless"—one which will entertain all time ("Centuries"), while her few stem glories will fade and her body will become an unknown mound in the dust. The final shocking image of beetles crawling about her grave serves as a harsh reminder of mortality and the failure of her infinite aspirations. The poem illustrates the permanence of eternal beauty against man's hopeless longing for these things. Although there is some significance in his attempt, his efforts to imitate the Divine necessarily fail. Man can be inspired by the handiwork of God, but ultimately he must perceive the indifference of nature and the transitory aspects of life which render these goals unobtainable. Man's mortality defeats him and the appalling distance between God and man remains.

Another Dickinson rephrasing of a biblical theme is "How happy is the little Stone." Like a Puritan minister she explicates the text, Luke 12:27, "Consider the lilies how they grow: they toil not, they spin not; and yet I say unto you, that Solomon in all his glory was not arrayed like one of these," and then applies it to the stone. Exploring the idea of nature's perfect harmony with the Divine plan, she contrasts the stone's elemental obedience with man's disordered existence. The poem revolves around these two poles of nature's simplicity and man's complexity, examining the relation of the inanimate stone to the cosmic order. The stone's simple aims and blind reliance upon universal law bring freedom and happiness. Since it never exceeds its limitations or potential, the stone achieves a rare self-sufficiency which mocks man's feverish careers and involved concerns. Throughout, the regular iambic tetrameter and fairly exact couplet rhyme exhibit the theme of restraint, or freedom within limits.

The satisfaction that results from the stone's close attunement to nature is presented from the opening lines. The stone is "happy" and wanders aimlessly, unconcerned about companionship and untouched by the complexities of human life. Even its fundamental

---

[2] Another reading for "Menagerie," given by Charles Anderson, is that they are her poetic attempts, which eventually will assure her immortality when she is physically dead. My over-all analysis of the poem greatly benefited from his explication.

brown color is the afterthought of a passing universe. But the stone's independence has an ironic side, since its freedom exists only within proscribed limits and without choice, thus being a mockery of the term. It associates merely by accident and is passively exposed to both warmth and cold. The irony of the poem is double-edged, for just as man's harried life seems hopelessly cluttered, the stone's casual existence is without value, for it involves no struggle. These qualities of freedom and responsibility make human life more perplexing and expose man to ridicule and failure, though they also allow personal achievement. "Consider the little stone," Emily Dickinson seems to say, "and see how man suffers by comparison." Still, the poem hints that perhaps man's dissatisfied struggle is better than the rote happiness of absolute decree.

A final example of her nature poetry is a treatment of the cricket in "Further in Summer than the Birds." The poem demonstrates again her fascination with nature's odd creatures and the mysterious passage of summer into winter. She once remarked that "Autumn is among us, though almost unperceived—and the Cricket sings in the morning, now, a most pathetic conduct," here as in the poem associating the cricket's song with the sadness of seasonal change. Basically the poem records the poet's response to the monotonous chirping of the crickets on a hot August noon near the end of summer. The tone throughout is hushed and solemn, imbued with a poignant sense of longing and awe by the pervasive religious undertones. The image of the cricket is transformed into a striking symbol of the estrangement and sorrow that man feels with the approach of winter: an echo of his own intimations of mortality.

> Further in Summer than the Birds
> Pathetic from the Grass
> A minor Nation celebrates
> Its unobtrusive Mass.

The insects exist "further" in summer than the birds because they live hidden in the soil close to nature's essence, while the birds build in the trees, inhabiting the sky and remaining longer into autumn. Unlike the beautiful lyrics of the birds, the crickets' song, produced by the rubbing together of their wings, is pathetic and often ignored. Their prophetic song is intimately related to their mating cycle for the males attract by this sound during their fall mating period. Also, the crickets' song is vitally dependent on temperature changes; when the temperature drops the crickets become sluggish and correspondingly their song diminishes. So, because of their passion's season, the majority of them die soon after the fall mating during the first protracted spell of freezing weather. In a sense, then, their mating foretells their coming death. So it can be compared to the sacrifice of the Mass, where Christ's love perpetuates the death sacrifice of Calvary by the transubstantiation of the bread and wine into his body and blood. The religious significance of the act is deepened by terms like "Ordinance," "Canticle," and "Druidic." The spoken "Mass," with its murmuring, barely audible Latin intonation, matches the steady, indistinguishable chirping of these insects.

> No Ordinance be seen
> So gradual the Grace
> A pensive Custom it becomes
> Enlarging Loneliness.

Yet the interested human listener is still alienated from the crickets' message. He can recognize no established rite for the administration of their sacrament ("Ordinance"), while the moral values signified by the ritual ("Grace") are barely understood. What does sound in the human soul is a "pensive Custom," one that saddens and brings introspection. The song of the crickets increases man's fundamental loneliness, since he is excluded from full participation in their ritual. In a sense, then, their song, as Yvor Winters has noted, demonstrates the cleavage of man from nature. Yet this "enlarging" also brings relief and comfort. Man finds his own estrangement from life echoed by nature itself, since the intensity of the insects' mating song ultimately foretells their death. Thus man can perceive that his isolation is not a unique phenomenon but cosmic and universal.

> Antiquest felt at Noon.
> When August burning low
> Arise this spectral Canticle
>
> .   .   .   .
>
> Remit as yet no Grace
> No Furrow on the Glow
> Yet a Druidic Difference
> Enhances Nature now

Widening the sacredness of the crickets' song ("Canticle"), Emily Dickinson definitely connects it with the harvest time. As the sun burns brightest and the crops fully ripen, the moment seems eternal. For this reason the time is most precious and most deeply felt ("Antiquest"). After such warmth and growth only cold and decay can follow in the cyclical pattern of nature. The crickets' song assumes a religious significance that typifies a temporary respite, the brief hesitation of the pendulum before it begins its downward sweep. The concluding lines enlarge this concept by noting that there is as yet no lessening of summer's beauty and abundance ("Grace"), nor any wrinkling or aging on its glow. Yet man's awareness of the song's foreboding implications, its connections with his own mortality, occasions a primitive sacredness ("Druidic") that makes the moment especially treasured.

Perhaps no other Dickinson poem has been subjected to such intensive criticism and controversy without any definitive statement concerning its full philosophical meanings. It will probably continue to fascinate as long as there are sensitive readers of poetry. And this seems true of all her best nature poems; they continually challenge and invite new readings. Her unique approach to the external beauty of nature, the power of storms, the strangeness of creation, the fleeting aspects of the material, and the mystery of the seasonal process fully demonstrate that even the most neglected and hackneyed subjects can be revitalized by genius.

6

SOCIAL SCENE AND LOVE

I F EMILY DICKINSON loved external nature and faithfully recorded her impressions of it, she was even more fascinated by the complex social scene around her. She responded to the interplay of community events and human personality, meditated on friendship, and closely examined her own deep experience of love and passion. Though she was detached from contemporary affairs and largely ignored momentous issues like the Civil War and slavery, she avidly read the *Springfield Republican, Scribners',* and the *Atlantic Monthly* and followed current literary figures like the Brontës, the Brownings, George Eliot, and Dickens. Her letters were studded with witty comments on local events and caricatures of Amherst inhabitants. She even satirized the newspapers' emphasis on disasters and crimes by asking Holland how an editor managed to get such humorous accounts of accidents and deaths written. For such an introspective writer, her poetry reflected a surprising variety of contemporary incidents—from balloon ascensions to circuses and railroads.

Since her father was one of the proud founders of the Amherst-Belchertown railroad, he functioned as "Chief Marshal" when the first train arrived in Amherst. However, his daughter, wryly amused at the pompous oratory and doubtful about the historic significance of the opening, later burlesqued the whole idea of the fabulous "iron horse" in "I like to see it lap the Miles." The conceit of the galloping horse is elaborated and exaggerated in the best tall-tale fashion. The breathless accumulation of action verbs ("lap," "lick," "stop," "feed," and "step" in the first stanza alone), the run-on lines, and the internal rhyme rush the poem to its panting finish. After describing the horse's difficulty in scraping through a quarry, she concludes:

> Complaining all the while
> In horrid—hooting stanza—
> Then chase itself down Hill—

And neigh like Boanerges—
Then—punctual as a Star
Stop—docile and omnipotent
At its own stable door—

The New Testament reference to Boanerges (Jesus' calling two of his zealous apostles "sons of thunder") and the incongruity of the beast's wild hooting being "punctual as a Star" deepen the humor of the train's neighing arrival at its stable-station.

This same fantastic tone guides the mock newspaper account of an attempted house robbery. "I know some lonely Houses off the Road" conveys a Tom Sawyer delight in haunted houses and mysterious treasure. A more imaginative treatment of local superstitions is "The only Ghost I ever saw." The tone throughout is that of a child's easy acceptance of the supernatural. The description of the ghost's mannerisms and personality suggest the ephemeral quality of the unknown. His clothes are fine Mechlin lace, his steps like snow flakes, and his manners are old-fashioned. Yet, in the final lines this shy, harmless figure is transformed into an appalling reality, which suggests the terror of death. So a child's fascinated response to the mysterious changes into fear, adding another dimension to this examination of the supernatural.

Like most New England towns, Amherst had its day of military training when the local militia drilled and paraded on the town common. The occasion attracted a crowd of onlookers, for the drill was often more humorous than military. In a short poem, "The Popular Heart is a Cannon First," Emily Dickinson used this colorful display, the rowdy mob, and the unruly drinking associated with the event to satirize unstable popular emotions. The second stanza more satirically depicts the drunken progress of democracy's defenders, who fall in ditches and finally end up in jail. Another poem on a crowd's fickleness ("You've seen Balloons set—Haven't You?") utilized the failure of a balloon ascension as the main image. Emily Dickinson probably never saw one, but during the middle nineteenth century public enthusiasm for such spectacles was intense. Newspaper accounts of the ascents were numerous, and she must have read some like the following from the *Springfield Republican* in 1860:

Precisely at 3 p.m., when the sky was clear and the face of nature warm and beautiful, the balloon of Mr. Spencer of Winstead, Ct., which had been inflated in front of the Mansion House, was cut loose from its moorings, and in the presence of thousands of specta-

77

tors rose rapidly . . . In less than ten minutes from leaving the earth, the balloon was invisible to the sea of upturned faces that gazed heavenward.

The poem contrasts the balloon's soaring, almost magical, ascent with the crowd's fickle response and disgust when the balloon crashes. Images of swans, diamond, and gold connote the balloon's ethereal beauty and highlight man's imaginative attempts to transcend his natural limitations. The crowd watches the event as curious onlookers at a side show, and their coarse disbelief signalizes their mean lives. They would not even encore death's appearance and so retire with an oath, while others remark that it was only a balloon falling. Various themes—the transitoriness of beauty, the indifference of human beings to suffering, the admirable, yet doomed attempts of man to conquer nature, or the tragic fall of a man from power—can be educed from the poem.

In a few poems Emily Dickinson deepened her nature sketches with social comment. "A Field of Stubble, lying sere" depicts the fallow, barren land after a fall harvest, while adding a human response to the scene. The farmer, taking the natural produce for food and profit, sees only the external scene and so misses the beauty and pathos inherent in the moment. The ending hints at the larger social tragedy of the post-Civil War, when New England farms were deserted for the rich lands of the Middle West.

One major area of community life that occupied her poetic imagination was, of course, death. Though she was principally concerned with death's physical and emotional effects, she also examined its external consequences, the changes in the household routine, the mourner's duties, the funeral services, even the cemetery itself. Her poems convey the total community response to death better than any social history. Combining the familiar with the awesome, she once described a coffin as an ordinary bed carefully made by a housewife, since the sleeper must rest in it until Judgment Day. In another poem, "Who occupies this House?" she achieves an even more difficult feat by creating light humor out of the graveyard scene. She avoids the grotesque, morbid humor usually associated with cemeteries and uses a naïve child's viewpoint to characterize the history and atmosphere of this strange town, with its citizens distinguished for their "gravity."

One of her best social comments on death is "There's been a Death, in the Opposite House." Here specific town customs, local manners, and dialect expressions elicit the hidden changes that death occasions. The colloquial tone of the opening stanzas, the use of a detached narrator interpreting all the casual "signs" for a puzzled visitor, and the imagistic development of the "numb" atmosphere exhibit Emily Dickinson's consummate genre skill in limning the social scene:

> There's been a Death, in the Opposite House,
> As lately as Today—
> I know it, by the numb look
> Such Houses have—alway—
>
> The Neighbors rustle in and out—
> The Doctor—drives away—
> A Window opens like a Pod—
> Abrupt—mechanically—

The second stanza contrasts society's ineffectual movements with the hush of death, while the window opening "like a Pod" startlingly interposes a familiar kitchen activity upon the death's strange stillness. The remainder of the poem enlarges the artificiality that death imposes upon life as the minister enters and then the undertaker (the man "of the Appalling Trade"), till finally the narrator observes that the "Dark Parade—/ Of Tassels—and of Coaches" will soon appear.

Yet the passing social panorama, with its funerals, balloon ascensions, and railroads, never attracted her like the actors themselves. Naturally, her own family performed daily before her amused eyes, though most of the observations on these shows were in prose. Her letters to Austin were crammed with witty, detached comments on her family's activities. An account of how her father read Austin's letters is typical:

> He reads all the letters you write as soon as he gets [them], at the post office, no matter to whom addressed. . . . He reads them once at the office, then he makes me read them loud at the supper table again, and when he gets home in the evening, he cracks a few walnuts, puts his spectacles on, and with your last in hand, sits down to enjoy the evening.

Truly a whole menagerie of people came under her lively surveillance, liberal ministers, evangelical preachers, drunkards, avaricious businessmen, town gossips, and the gentlewomen of Amherst. With portraits etched in acid she caricatured Amherst inhabitants as Edwin Arlington Robinson was later to capture the Tilbury townspeople. "He preached upon 'Breadth' till it argued him narrow" satirizes the learned preacher who lectures about truth and values without any insight into the spiritual. Another poem, "He fumbles at your

Soul," graphically records her emotional response to a revival sermon and even equals Jonathan Edwards' "Narrative of Surprising Conversions" in capturing the rapturous excitement occasioned by an evangelical meeting. The poem conveys the "holy kind of violence" that an influx of grace brings, describing the slow emotional buildup as the soul reluctantly responds, wavers with doubts, and then suddenly surrenders. The final moment of ecstasy is pain-filled and wrenching, since the material world has to be overwhelmed before the spiritual can triumph.[1]

A final group of poems that satirize the sterile minds and petty attitudes of Amherst ladies is best illustrated by "What Soft—Cherubic Creatures." Here Emily Dickinson mocks the conventional lives of these gentlewomen, whose overrefinement denies natural emotions and the essence of Christianity. The principal images compare the women to soft plush and brittle stars, signifying their weakness and breakable veneer surface.

> What Soft—Cherubic Creatures—
> These Gentlewomen are—
> One would as soon assault a Plush—
> Or violate a Star—

The opening lines are deceptive, since "soft" indicates womanly tenderness and loving qualities, while "cherubic" implies religious traits. However, the remainder of the stanza undercuts these associations to emphasize the overly weak natures and unformed, decorative characteristics of these women. The sexual associations in "assault" and "violate" shock when applied to these gentlewomen. Any emotion, much less a passionate one, is completely foreign to their natures. The soft assonance and "s" alliteration center on "plush," a velvety material that signifies their yielding, doughlike character. The "star" comparison is apt, since they are distant and aloof, glittering with an icy brilliance that is alien in a human world.

> Such Dimity Convictions—
> A Horror so refined
> Of freckled Human Nature—
> Of Deity—ashamed—
>
> It's such a common—Glory—
> A Fisherman's—Degree—
>
> . . . .

[1] Clark Griffith in his *The Long Shadow: Emily Dickinson's Tragic Poetry* has an extensive analysis of the sexual and erotic implications contained in the poem.

The second and third stanzas expand these two concepts. The ladies, no longer creatures, are now "convictions" and a finely woven cotton cloth ("Dimity"). The pun in "Dimity" on their size and lack of intelligence is an ironic link with their "star" quality, something dimly seen by human eyes. Even their refined "Horror" is mocked, since it is a fear of the sun freckling their white skin. They are afraid of ordinary human nature, which is necessarily soiled by original sin, and so deny Christ who came in poverty for these commoners. The last stanza completes the damning portrait. As if parodying their languid, bored tone, Emily Dickinson notes that they call Christ's divine mission a "common—Glory." She intimates that they would be ashamed of the rough, unschooled fishermen whom Christ hand-picked for his first apostles. The final image of "Brittle Lady" picks up the "Star-Dimity" concept and warns that their denial of human nature will cause Christ to reject them. Throughout, their artificial lives are contrasted with the natural, human warmth of Christianity. Underlying the whole poem is the idea that the spirit, not the letter of the law, saves.

The Amherst social scene and its inhabitants were only a minor grouping among her poems dealing with the effect of love on human relations. Her own experience of passion occasioned most of her love poetry, but she also considered the subject from a philosophical viewpoint. The extravagance of her feelings about love's importance caused her to remark that "love is all there is" and to equate it with God himself. Because love was meaningless unless reciprocated, she felt that God was dependent upon man's love for complete happiness. The concept was hardly Christian, for it assumed that God was not perfect, but continually evolving. Love triumphs over both life and death to achieve an almost divine status. One of her poems, "Till Death—is narrow Loving," states that only death's separation truly measures the extent of love. As she matured, she realized that love created the only harmony in the universe and that divine love surpassed nature's beauty and human affection.

Concerning friendship she was equally ecstatic, writing that: "My friends are my 'estate.' Forgive me then the avarice to hoard them! They tell me those were poor early, have different views of gold. I dont know how that is. God is not so wary as we, else he would give us no friends, lest we forget him!" However, few of her poems on the subject have literary merit. "The Soul selects her own Society" is the one main exception:

> The Soul selects her own Society—
> Then—shuts the Door—
> To her divine Majority—
> Present no more—
>
> . . . .
>
> I've known her—from an ample nation—
> Choose One—
> Then—close the Valves of her attention—
> Like Stone—

The keynote of the poem is the exclusiveness of friendship, the highly selective quality of affection. Religious and regal associations are combined with images of enclosure to emphasize the soul's individuality. The opening lines portray the soul's careful survey of the "ample nation" for suitable society. In much the same manner as God "elects" or saves his chosen saints, the privilege of friendship is conferred on few, and ultimately only one person receives it. The image of the closed door conveys the utter finality of her choice and is later reflected by the archaic meaning of "Valves," the two leaves of a double door. Condensation renders the next two lines somewhat obscure, but one reading is that, after selecting the chosen friend, the soul dramatically denies all others as a symbol of her now matured life ("divine Majority"). She has come of spiritual and emotional age and no longer needs to "present" herself to the world. The second stanza contrasts this inner security with the attempts of Emperors to win her affection. The metric shift in "Choose One" and the image of valves closing like stone intensify her exclusiveness. The valves not only expand the door image but, as a mechanical connection that stops or allows the flow of emotions, they also indicate the soul's impervious control. The poem ends harshly as the image of the impenetrable, unfeeling stone reflects the soul's attitude toward other claimants for her affections.

Before tracing the pattern of Emily Dickinson's well-known love poems, we should examine a unique, often ignored grouping.[2] These poems, far more disturbing than her other love lyrics, investigate the tremendous emotional influence exerted by the male upon the passive female. They emphasize the power of physical attraction and the fear of passionate response within an allegorical framework. One of the lighter ones, "I started Early—Took my Dog," has a childlike surface story. A young girl visits the seashore, gets her

---

[2] Clark Griffith is one of the few critics who has extensively handled these poems of emotional frustration and sexual attraction. His book contains revealing discussions of "I started Early—Took my Dog" and "In Winter in my Room."

shoes wet, and then, cold and frightened, runs home. The droll images, "Hempen Hands," "Dandelion's Sleeve," and "Silver Heel," and the fantastic situation contribute to a fairy-tale mood.

> I started Early—Took my Dog—
> And visited the Sea—
> The Mermaids in the Basement
> Came out to look at me—

The girl begins her journey "Early," presumably because the trip is hazardous and not often attempted. "Early" also signifies her un-formed, impressionable nature, which matures by the end of the poem. As a hesitant caller before royalty she senses the strangeness of her position, being disdained by mermaids, whose basement homes allude to her own abandoned security. These half-human, half-fish creatures combine both sea and land qualities. Perhaps they were once young girls like her who ventured too near the Sea and were transformed by his power. The second stanza intensifies her sense of isolation, her being aground "upon the Sands." The land's daily routine and conventions still grasp her feet, as she takes the last steps toward the Sea. Stanzas three and four deepen these under-tones as her early excitement turns to uneasiness and then outright fear. The water covers her shoes and then metaphorically moves past her apron and bodice. The mild sexual imagery and the dream-like mood indicate her entranced fascination with the Sea's advances. Yet, her newly awakened emotions are shaken by his attempt at complete possession and fearfully she turns and runs.

> And He—He followed—close behind—
> I felt his Silver Heel
> Upon my Ankle—Then my Shoes
> Would overflow with Pearl—
>
> Until We met the Solid Town—
> No One He seemed to know—
> And bowing—with a Mighty look—
> At me—the Sea withdrew—

The repetitious "And He—He" underscores her shock at his bold-ness and her own willingness to allow such freedom. Unlike a con-ventional Amherst boy who would apologize once he was rebuffed, the Sea merely renews his advances. Though her surprise turns into terror, the beauty of his "Silver Heel" and "Pearl" still attract. In the last stanza she makes her frightened escape by returning to the town she so eagerly left that morning. Now she is safe, but at the price of the Sea's withdrawn, regal disdain. The final lines echo her loss and isolation, as she senses what she has rejected. Certainly the trip can be viewed as her pathetic effort to leave the "sand"-bound town for the fluid freedom of the sea. Also it hints of a movement from childhood through the maturity of a difficult trip to a final confrontation with death, which causes terror and retreat. Examining all the associations clustered about the Sea, his beauty, freedom, haughtiness, male power, and the shy, fearful, repressed qualities of the female and the land, the poem is perhaps best read as the emotional and physical effects of a lover's advances. She nearly succumbs, but her life of control and suppression proves stronger and she returns to the "solid" town. The basic theme is the rejection of one of life's prime forces—love, sex, beauty, or death—for a weak, conventional existence.

A far more disturbing poem is "In Winter in my Room." Here a graphic description of sexual attraction combined with an analysis of the fascination and fear it arouses renders the poem a classic pre-Freudian study of repressed desire. Her rejection of the physical and her conclusion that "this was a dream" illustrate how the conscious mind, the ego, denies and rejects the surging drives of the subconscious id. Again the mood is made childlike by repeated, suspended rhyme and short trimeter lines. The basic story is more allegorical than "I started Early—Took my Dog." A woman finds a small, harmless worm in her room and decides to keep it tied to her apron strings. Suddenly it changes into a powerful snake that threatens her, causing her flight to another town.

> In Winter in my Room
> I came upon a Worm—
> Pink, lank and warm—
>
> . . . .
> Secured him by a string
> To something neighboring

The opening scene is in winter, in the frozen dead state of her emotions, and in her room where she is secure and protected from any change. Yet a small worm intrudes upon her isolation, and its harmless babylike condition wins her affection, though the image also has phallic suggestions that are later expanded. Despite her maternal attraction she is aware of the worm's deceitful nature and so cautiously ties him to her apron strings. Her attempts to tame and control the explosive male force demonstrate her naïveté, for soon afterward the worm does turn and she discovers:

84

A snake with mottles rare
Surveyed my chamber floor
In feature as the worm before
But ringed with power—

Now a powerful snake, it dominates her room and with a sure power and beauty holds her fascinated attention. She is stunned by the change but still tries to appease and control the snake (" 'How fair you are!' / Propitiation's claw"). Though terrified, her first words reveal the attraction of his physical beauty. In the ensuing dialogue the snake toys with her, trying to soothe her suspicions until:

Then to a Rhythm *Slim*
Secreted in his Form
As Patterns swim
Projected him.

As if words were meaningless, he makes his final appeal from the source of his power, the coiled, deadly rhythm of a snake about to strike, which parallels rising sexual desire. Torn by her repulsion and attraction, she wavers, only to retreat suddenly to a new town, determinedly maintaining that this was all a dream. The allegorical framework seems quite clear. A soul in the depths of emotional stagnation finds a companion ("worm") whom she can mother and love without fear. Yet the relationship alters as her emotional response overwhelms the friendly love and the worm-turned-snake breaks her controlling bonds. His direct advances bring pleasure and free her repressed emotions, but she still temporizes. Though swayed by his appeal, she cannot shake her fears and so she retreats into her former isolated state. Trying to banish even the memory of her desire and emotional crisis, she states "this was a dream."

A final poem in this group, "My Life had stood—a Loaded Gun," is perhaps her best poetic statement about the explosive changes that passion wrought on her emotions. The central conceit of a loaded gun connotes a potential, inert force, one with explosive power, which can only be released by another. The concept of the active male hunter possessing the passive woman guides the whole poem. Once he leaves, she reverts to her inactive gun state.

My Life had stood—a Loaded Gun—
In Corners—till a Day
The Owner passed—identified—
And carried Me away—

> And now We roam in Sovereign Woods—
> And now We hunt the Doe—
> And every time I speak for Him—
> The Mountains straight reply—

Her life is described as a loaded gun, filled with emotional force and sensitivity, but standing forsaken in a pawnshop waiting for redemption. The owner merely has to show his ticket in order to carry her away. So their fated love casts her in the role of a passive force that only he can release from a stagnant life. Now a balladlike mood depicts her romantic fulfillment as the "we," united in love and purpose, hunt a regal domain searching for game and things of beauty ("Doe"). Their relationship is not entirely one-sided, for he needs her destructive power. Without her the hunter is incomplete, but now his slightest touch causes her to explode and command mountains for him. Stressing her emotional response and unleashed destructive power, the next three stanzas emphasize the pleasure she gives him, the protection she renders him at night, and the revenge she wreaks upon his enemies. Yet significantly the line "Our good Day done" hints that their hunting union is at an end. She further comments on her desire to guard his bed rather than share its physical pleasure. These changes prepare for the perplexing and somewhat obscure final stanza.

> Though I than He—may longer live
> He longer must—than I—
> For I have but the power to kill,
> Without—the power to die—

This appears to mean that at death he has a chance for spiritual salvation and immortality. But his domination has so exhausted her spirit that she is lifeless and inert without his love. His complete possession and her submission to his least command leave her, upon his departure, without the right or desire to "die" in a religious sense. She must remain passive and unfulfilled, abandoned in a pawnshop with only the unused power to kill, but without the right to die into immortal life. These final lines introduce a spiritual perspective to catch the pathos of her doomed life.

Apart from these psychological studies of repression and emotional desire, the majority of her love poems more openly handle the effects of passion upon a human soul. Not least among the many ironies of her relationship with Higginson was his public comment that no American writer has ever written great love poetry and that "the American poet of passion is yet to come"—and this after having read some of her love poems. Certainly few American poets before or since had been so concerned with describing the effects of love and passion. Unfortunately most of her love poems are so tortured and so intimately related to her deepest feelings that they lack the artistic control necessary to raise them beyond the biographical and the personal. Three principal motifs can be discerned in these poems: the anticipation of the lover's future visit and possible marriage; the climactic meeting of the lovers and their resulting separation; and finally the sublimation of the human passion in a celestial marriage as she becomes the Bride of Christ.

The first grouping contains her most sentimental and derivative love poems. Some deal with erotic expectations, employing the bee-flower image to convey physical desire as in "Come slowly—Eden!" and "A Bee his burnished Carriage"; others with longing for imagined visits, "If you were coming in the Fall"; and some with an abstract examination of transport and awe like " 'Tis so much joy! 'Tis so much joy!" Two poems convey her exultation and triumph as she imagines herself a true wife and boasts of the superhuman intensity of her passion. "I'm ceded—I've stopped being Theirs," though closely related to her Bride of Christ poems, emphasizes the actual attainment of the wife status. The poem contrasts the two sacraments of baptism and marriage: her church baptism as a help-less infant in the arms of her father, where the sacrament was merely external and unwanted; and her new, mature crowning as a woman in marriage, where the baptism was freely chosen and elevated her to queenhood. Baptism and coronation motifs are artistically interwoven and blended with suggestive hints of sexual surrender to capture a woman's exuberant happiness on the day of her marriage. "Dare you see a Soul *at the White Heat?*" lacks the intricate struc-ture of "I'm ceded—I've stopped being Theirs," but stands as a more moving emotional utterance. It passionately taunts the on-looker to view the searing intensity of her love without being blinded. She says that red is love's usual sign, but that her passion has vanquished this to blaze at white heat. The unhallowed fire of secular love and the holocaust of suffering have so perfected her soul that she is now ready for God's immortal light. The poem's vivid "forge" imagery dramatically stresses the strength of this earthly love, which transforms her emotional experience into a divine readi-ness for immortality or heaven.

The largest grouping among her love poems is composed of those concerned with the actual meeting of the lovers. Usually recollected from the vantage point of separation and with the realization of the love's termination, they are dominated by a haunting sense of anguish. They constantly emphasize her sense of loyalty and dread of change and increasingly consider the spiritual aspects of love, rather than its human importnce.[3] "Again—his voice is at the door" is typical, being an exact recounting of a sublime emotional moment when two human beings are united by love. However, this brief ecstasy leaves the lover savoring the moment in a desperate attempt to make memory serve for reality. The opening stanzas, with their biographical suggestions, are the most moving.

"There came a Day at Summer's full" views a similar experience from a religious perspective, one that boldly assumes that the lovers' earthly renunciation will gain them heavenly bliss. However, the poem is not basically religious, for she insists, even demands, that their temporary ecstasy and long separation portend a greater spiritual happiness. God is curiously absent from the poem as she considers heaven acceptable only if it fully consummates their love. Here the loss is accepted, not because denial is beneficial, but because it must bring eternal, perfect union.

By contrast, "I got so I could take his name" catches the terrible misery that the separation causes, depicting the soul's bleak efforts to discover some measure of religious consolation. The poet finds no assurance in conventional religions; her direct appeal to God for solace remains unanswered. The first three stanzas convey the pain of renunciation and the tensions of the final meeting better than any of her other love poems:

> I got so I could take his name—
> Without—Tremendous gain—
> That Stop-sensation—on my Soul—
> And Thunder—in the Room—
>
> I got so I could walk across
> That Angle in the floor,
> Where he turned so, and I turned—how—
> And all our Sinew tore—
>
> I got so I could stir the Box—
> In which his letters grew
> Without that forcing, in my breath—
> As Staples—driven through—

[3] The following list is a brief selection from scores of these poems. Though uneven and too personal, they have many sections of great lyric beauty and merit reading: "The Way I read a Letter's—this," "I cannot live with You," "Although I put away his life," "I live with Him—I see His face," "You said

The idiomatic "I got so" indicates her qualified acceptance of the loss, a position still tenuous and unstable, while "take" suggests the sacredness of his name, as if one profaned by using it. The dashes after "name" and "without" provide a pause before the overwhelming effects of his love explode in "Tremendous gain," "Stop-sensation," and "Thunder." The second stanza recounts their agonized last meeting and focuses on the implications of "turn." Their physical withdrawal signifies a parallel "turn" into renunciation and suggests an eventual turn to the spiritual hope of the final stanzas. The exact description of the angle in the floor brilliantly reworks the sentimental clichés of treasuring locks of hair and faded rose buds, while the translation of the lovers' emotional misery into real physical pain ("Sinew tore") indicates the depth of their passion. The third stanza alters the mood. As the memory of the meeting dims, she desperately strives to re-experience the former ecstasy, even to feel the despairing pain, by touching his letters. The word "stir" signifies her pathetic attempts to make the letters serve for his physical presence. The contrast of the listless "stir" with the vibrant excitement of his former visits reveals the gradual alteration that passing time brings. The image of the staples being driven through dramatizes the "Stop-sensation" of the opening stanza as his iron male force cuts through and forever binds her inert "page" life. The remainder of the poem treats the present, where she hopelessly seeks some religious answer. The final lines picture God as too distant, "too vast," to even care about "so minute affair / As Misery."

A final poem in this group, "I should have been too glad, I see," marks a transition into her Bride of Christ poems, although the emotional splendor of her secular love modulates its religious emphasis. Here the religious consolation so eagerly sought in the previous poem is more satisfactorily explored. In a sense, the poem is an elaborate rationalization, an attempt to explain why the love was denied. She argues that their relationship was so sublime and so complete that it endangered their love for God. Thus God removed this paradise on earth to reassert his value and to allow them a chance for spiritual happiness. The ironic phrasing and her own pleading tone indicate that this resignation is still somewhat forced. After listing consoling axioms and using the comparison of the crucifixion followed by Easter, she still concludes that one has

that I 'was Great'—one Day," "You constituted Time," "Because that you are going," "Somewhere upon the general Earth," and "The most pathetic thing I do."

difficulty in understanding and obtaining belief. The quotation marks around "faith" (as if it were found in some forgotten volume) and the image of the wounded animal crying out in anguish suggest that faith has brought little relief. The first stanza indicates the general approach. Using status images, she immediately presents the dilemma. With the continuance of her love she would have been exalted far beyond the minor role that this transitory life had arranged for her. The Calvinistic concept of life as pain-filled, with the only happiness dependent upon an omnipotent God, underscores this whole passage. Deprecatingly she asserts that her insignificant life, which is hardly worthy of the happiness she was experiencing, would have eventually embarrassed this perfect love, which is religious as well as emotional. If it had continued, she would have been critical of all other remaining moments. The extreme condensation of these lines renders interpretation difficult. The next two stanzas expand these ideas, showing that her profane love would have obliterated the sacred and would have eliminated the fear of hell so necessary for securing heaven. The final stanza is the weakest, as somehow the conventional platitudes that should render solace do not bring faith or acceptance.

Her most artistic love poems are those dealing with brides and marriage. As the realization of the lover's loss deepened and as his physical presence became mere memory, she gradually sublimated her human passion into a divine experience. In this new cycle of poems the human lover remains shadowy as her vision of the lovers' heavenly marriage changes to an actual celestial union with God. Like Edward Taylor and other religious poets, she dramatically merges the sacred and profane aspects of human passion, transforming her desire for human marriage into a Bride of Christ vision. Throughout most of these poems the term "bride" is viewed from various perspectives: first as an actual woman being married; then as the bride of death, which allows her to enter the third stage as wedded to God in paradise. Charles Anderson notes:

> The struggle between earthly and heavenly love remains central to the most successful poems in the marriage group. More accurately it is the source of the tension she sets up by embodying the heavenly theme in earthly terms, then making these into images with celestial reference. . . . Two strategies of language are responsible for this success, the language of Status and the Signs which denote the elevation from one level to another.

The adjustment to the idea of a divine lover was gradual, and in the beginning she insists that after a long separation the heavenly lovers will celebrate a spiritual marriage before angelic hosts.[4] "Of all the Souls that stand create" is perhaps the best among the many poems dealing with this heavenly marriage. It uses the framework of the Last Judgment to assert triumphantly the validity of her choice. After such pain and denial she is convinced that eternity will vindicate her selection. Interwoven throughout the poem is the basic contrast between temporal life, characterized by images of obscurity and heaviness, and eternity's strength and clarity. She claims that she has chosen the best, the one soul whose value can be recognized only in eternity. Again utilizing the doctrine of election and God's irresistible grace, she finally cries out for all to view the one person, the atom, she has chosen. This fits the imagistic pattern of election, since the atom was then thought to be the ultimate indissoluble element of matter, and its unique, eternal characteristics contrast with the damp, moldable clay of most lives. Yet a touch of irony exists, for what she claims finally is only an atom, a small insignificant particle, one among millions.

Emily Dickinson's particular success in capturing the exultation and passionate satisfaction that renunciation brings is nowhere better displayed than in the following poem:

> Mine—by the Right of the White Election!
> Mine—by the Royal Seal!
> Mine—by the Sign in the Scarlet prison—
>
> . . . .
>
> Mine—here—in Vision—and in Veto!
> Mine—by the Grave's Repeal—
> Titled—Confirmed—
> Delirious Charter!
> Mine—long as Ages steal!

Just what is hers is never fully explained, but from the total sense of achievement one assumes that her mastery of pain has conferred upon her a special divine privilege, a marriage deed to eternity. The repeated assertion of "Mine" creates a rising rhetorical pattern, where the explanation of how she obtained her new rank also defines what this "Delirious Charter" is. "Right" and "White Election" present the key images of legal sanction and orthodox religious salvation which guide the whole poem. She merits this new estate as one

---

[4] Other bridal poems that are not considered in this section, but that repay reading are: "I'm 'wife'—I've finished that," "A solemn thing—it was—I said," "A Wife—at Daybreak I shall be," " 'Twas a long Parting—but the time," and "She rose to His Requirement—dropt."

who has argued her case before the bar or who has been specially saved. "White" has the secular association with bridal gowns and refers to her own symbolic use of the color, besides alluding to the saved figures in white who appear before the Lamb of God in the book of Revelation. "By the Royal Seal" expands the legal concept with the hint of royalty and suggests a marriage ring or license. The next two lines refer to her own tortured suffering, by which she merits this special privilege. Also, they vaguely allude to Christ's passion, which is more openly reflected in "Grave's Repeal." Like Miriam's song of victory over the Egyptians, the second stanza intensifies the "Mine" into a cry of jubilation. The cryptic first line implies that this "White Election" is hers "here" on earth because of her denial of human love ("in Veto"), but that she has this rank only in a spiritual sense ("in Vision"). This present state almost rivals immortality and is further paralleled by Christ's resurrection, which forever proved his divinity. The final lines transform the official ceremony into an ecstatic vision, and the poem concludes with eternity giving its majestic approval to her charter.

A companion poem, which more inherently blends spiritual love and human passion, is "Title divine—is mine!" Here the ritual of an actual marriage without the human bridegroom is so fully developed that one can almost feel the human passion being transformed into divine love. The rich cluster of images dealing with precious stones, royalty, and status intensify the poem's marriage theme:

> Title divine—is mine!
> The Wife—without the Sign!
> Acute Degree—conferred on me—
> Empress of Calvary!

The opening lines defiantly vaunt her triumph with an exultation that the internal rhyme makes almost childishly boastful. In this poem the achievement is clarified and expressed as a "Title divine," a wife without the external symbols, rings, dresses, and ceremony, common to most brides. Her marriage is different, one so keenly felt that it brings both pleasure and pain. Her rejection of an earthly marriage has made her an "Empress" of suffering, worthy to be the Bride of Christ. The term "Calvary" also has biographical significance, since this was the name of the church in California where Charles Wadsworth became pastor in the year the poem was written.

The middle section expands this imagery. She is royal though lacking a crown and betrothed without the usual swoon romantically associated with utmost happiness. The lines "Garnet to Garnet—/

Gold to Gold" symbolize wedding pledges and rings that officially seal the marriage and suggest a physical union. The concluding lines read:

> Born—Bridalled—Shrouded—
> In a Day—
> Tri Victory
> "My Husband"—women say—
> Stroking the Melody—
> Is *this*—the way?

The heavily accentuated first syllables intensify the thought. A bride is born to new life in marriage, "Bridalled," since she is subordinated to her husband (the pun is a typical Dickinson touch), and "Shrouded," since her virgin life is now dead. On a spiritual level, this indicates that her complete submission to Christ transcends all of physical life in an instant ("In a Day"). The final lines wistfully dream of an actual marriage as she imagines new brides rapturously caressing the sound of "My Husband." An ironic note creeps into "Is *this*—the way," as if her possession of Christ's love renders earthly marriage insignificant. Yet the lines are ambiguous, implying envy as well as disdain. Appropriately the poem ends with this delicate suggestion of the pain and pleasure that accompanies both states.

The blend of passion and sacred love in these two poems is climaxed by another poem, "Given in Marriage unto Thee," which banishes actual marriage for a complete heavenly union. Now there is no hint of human love, only the beatific serenity of a nun voicing her vows to the bridegroom Christ. Certainly America had found the poet of passion that Higginson claimed it needed. No other nineteenth-century American poet, neither Whitman with his open celebration of sexual attraction nor Poe with his ethereal lines on doomed beauty, ever equaled the intensity of her love lyrics. She imbued her personal attachment with a religious significance that transformed biography into art. Her social and love lyrics illustrate her continual movement into the domain of human affairs. From the external world of nature she passed to social satire and finally to the intimate realm of love and passion. The stage is now set for her presentation of love's connection with pain and death.

7

PAIN AND DEATH

If HUMAN LOVE and supernal bliss were one side of life's coin, the reverse showed pain and loss. Of course, many of Emily Dickinson's love lyrics dealt with renunciation to demonstrate how pain could transform passion into spiritual love. Beyond these love-pain lyrics another poetic grouping investigated the nature of pain, its stages, its effects upon the human soul, and finally its relation with death. She gradually learned how to master the pain of separation and in time analyzed the experience with artistic detachment. The resulting poems not only enabled her to weather the pain and to preserve her integrity but also helped turn deprivation into a spiritual triumph. In total they constituted a revealing illustration of one soul's courage.

Since these poems dealing with misery, anguish, and despair were so closely related to her philosophy of life, her concept of the soul must be considered. Introspection came naturally to this child of Calvinism who was taught its intense concern for inner reality, while a love for precise definition was absorbed from her family's legal tradition. Like Jonathan Edwards, she wrote her own "Notes on the Mind," though they were expressed in poetry, not prose.

> This Consciousness that is aware
> Of Neighbors and the Sun
> Will be the one aware of Death
> And that itself alone
>
> Is traversing the interval
> Experience between
> And the most profound experiment
> Appointed unto Men—

Primarily she observes that death brings no sudden change, for just as one lives, so one experiences death. Though the soul exists in a natural world of "Sun" and social contact, the inner world of self views life in solitude and faces death unaided and alone. As Thomas

Johnson in his critical biography has observed about this poem: "Such consciousness is uniquely the property of each individual. A man's soul is an identity that can never be known to others or shared by them. The adventure of living, wherein our souls are placed in mortal frames, condemns us to solitude." Paradoxically the poem concludes by remarking that life, though a fascinating adventure, is an experience that the soul endures by the mere accident of birth. She constantly explored the mind's peculiar workings ("A Thought went up my mind today"), estimated its powers ("The Brain—is wider than the Sky"), and contrasted its perceptions with actual experience ("The Brain, within it's Groove"). Her adventure into the hidden self led to the ultimate perception that there is no absolute answer for life's problems. She felt that living was an education which one accepted, even though it was unexpected and often unwanted. In one poem, "Experience is the Angled Road," she says that the mind thinks of reality in one way, while experience is often quite the opposite. Reality is a twisting, difficult road that is finally preferred over the mind because it is closer to the truth. Ironically she notes that the mind hopes to reach some preconceived good, only to discover that its theory differs from reality.

She realized that all experiences were relative and determined by their context. Time changes pain; love reflects a person's mood; the eye creates beauty; and the precious quality of life depends on its mortality. Many of her poems, for example, "Success," deal with the laws of compensation and the interrelation of pleasure and pain, ecstasy and despair. She viewed both sides of an experience and, unhindered by dogma or traditional concepts, accepted life as it occurred. Unflinchingly she faced its misery and loneliness, even relishing its bitterness, since this too was an aspect of life. Sometimes she claimed that anticipation surpassed attainment and that pain alone endured while happiness was denied. Yet she never ceased her struggle, nor allowed any facet of pain to escape her acute observation.

Complementing her belief in compensation was her awareness that pain and denial qualified all experiences. For Emily Dickinson as for Hawthorne and James the knowledge of pain became a touchstone for estimating the depth of a human soul. No sham survived misery's terrible stress. "I measure every Grief I meet" presents her philosophy of pain and analyzes its specific characteristics. Primarily she notes that true pain becomes such an essential part of one's being that its departure causes a deeper loneliness in the soul. Since pain's intensity is unrelenting, one can never master it, nor even hope for time to assuage its power. Yet pain has value, since it provides the victim with an enlightenment to a "larger Pain." That is, from a personal experience of grief one comes to the realization of its universal human condition. Thus, it greatly strengthens man, enabling him to bear increased stresses and survive as an individual. In her poems pain almost assumes the legendary proportions of death. The poem closes with:

> A piercing Comfort it affords
> In passing Calvary—
>
> To note the fashions—of the Cross—
> And how they're mostly worn—
> Still fascinated to presume
> That Some—are like My Own—

Thus pain elevates man to new heights, establishing an aristocratic bond with others who experience similar anguish. Her belief in the abiding nature of pain reflects basic Calvinistic doctrine and indicates her break with Transcendental optimism. Though her struggle re-affirmed man's inner greatness, she remained uncertain of final victory over these disintegrating forces.

Many of her poems on pain dealt with the moment after a near disaster, the very second when a soul has passed through the terrible abyss of the unknown or death's annihilation. Poor organization and shifting metaphors mar the majority of these poems, but sections hauntingly evoke a soul's collapse under extreme pressures. They reflect Emily Dickinson's preoccupation with moments of change and her fascination with the borderline between life and death. " 'Twas like a Maelstrom, with a notch" describes the psychological shock of a soul saved from imminent destruction by a mere whim of God. Prepared for disaster, the soul miraculously survives, only to realize that the continuing pain will bring renewed torture. Paradoxically, salvation appears no better than death. The opening description of the maelstrom aptly illuminates the nightmarish quality of the experience, but the other metaphors lack dramatic effectiveness. Throughout the poem one senses how close to madness pain has pushed this soul.

"It was not Death, for I stood up" more artistically examines the state of shock and numbness that extreme grief causes. The pattern of the poem reflects the chaos of tortured emotions and the wretchedness of despair. Only a series of negations can describe what the soul suffers. The experience is neither death nor life, cold nor warmth, noon nor midnight, but fragments of them all that enlarge the soul's terror. She ransacked her poetic imagination to express suitably these sensations and finally let images of death, night, and coldness convey despair's effect:

> It was not Death, for I stood up,
> And all the Dead, lie down—
> It was not Night, for all the Bells
> Put out their Tongues, for Noon.

The negation of one state is immediately followed by its opposite to widen the anguish of the total experience. These disjointed remarks manifest the soul's dazed attempt to master the tensions destroying its balance. Funereal images dominate the central section and somewhat morbidly equate her experience to a corpse's being shaved and fitted in the coffin. She exhibits the soul's terrible desolation by comparing its state to midnight, to staring space, and finally to "Grisly frosts—first Autumn morns,/ Repeal[ing] the Beating Ground." This striking metaphor compares the slow pulse of life still throbbing in her numbed body to seeds covered by the death of winter and ice. The final stanza employs a shipwreck image to illustrate the chaos and hopelessness of despair:

> But, most, like Chaos—Stopless—cool—
> Without a Chance, or Spar—
> Or even a Report of Land—
> To justify—Despair.

Another poem, "The first Day's Night had come," considers the courage required to endure an initial shock and the relief in mastering the first day's pain. However, when another day of pain comes the mind collapses, realizing that this same effort must be made daily for the rest of its life. "That after Horror—that 'twas *us*," the final poem in this category, more closely relates to her love life than the others. It also describes the numbed responses of a soul, reeling from the horror of near disaster. The italicized "us" of the poem implies that a deceptively stable relationship came close to disaster (possibly a near succumbing to passion) and was barely salvaged by a moral force ("Savior"). The central metaphor builds on the paradox of external strength and security hiding weakness and instability. The first stanza captures the mixture of good and evil possible in human relationships:

> That after Horror—that 'twas *us*—
> That passed the mouldering Pier—
> Just as the Granite Crumb let go—
> Our Savior, by a Hair—

97

The poem opens with the stunned pair surveying the thin margin of their escape. The apparently solid pier upon which their relationship rests is actually decayed and collapses beneath the first serious pressure. The "Granite Crumb" image expands this "pier" concept, for the solid granite stone has a crumb's weakness. The image suggests a tombstone's falling into a sunken grave, while the "let go" implies their total abandonment. The second stanza reiterates the idea of a sudden fall, also hinting at Christ's saving grace ("A second more, had dropped too deep/ For Fisherman to plumb"). To convey the terror of this escape, the poet shifts her viewpoint to contemplate what an entrance into "Conjecture's presence" (God) would have been like without hope of salvation.

Many of these poems on pain bypassed its underlying causes to examine pain's physical and emotional effects. Rather than dealing with extreme psychological tension, they stressed the courage required to endure the burdens of pain. Once the initial shock receded the more difficult task of living with this death-in-life began. In "I dreaded that first Robin, so" the soul waits for external nature to mirror its misery, only to observe all the beauties of spring unfolding to mock her bereaved state. Noting that not a single blossom sympathetically defers to her martyrdom, she concludes that nature is basically indifferent and man is isolated from its harmony. Here an ironic tone freshens the pathetic fallacy. "I tie my Hat—I crease my Shawl" also exemplifies Emily Dickinson's genre skill in allowing insignificant details to highlight the bleak courage required when all reason for living has gone. Her New England stoicism and Puritan resolution force her to closely measure this pain and by her courageous endurance make this wasted life assume nobility.

One of her best definition poems attempts to explain the effect of renunciation. Basically the poem explores the "piercing" results of surrendering an immediate presence for a vague expectation. The measured iambic pentameter lines are split into jagged fragments, while the irregular rhyme manifests the agony and dislocation that renunciation brings. The structure of the poem moves from an external analysis of what renunciation involves to a consideration of the soul's inner struggle:

> Renunciation—is a piercing Virtue—
> The letting go
> A Presence—for an Expectation—
> Not now—
> The putting out of Eyes—

> Just Sunrise—
> Lest Day—
> Day's Great Progenitor—
> Outvie

The word "Renunciation" implies a formal giving up of a right, a virtue only a superior soul can achieve. Since this act cruelly denies the soul's yearning, it can be exercised only in a ceremonial pattern. What renunciation involves is the "letting go" (a phrase that suggests a tenacious grasp) of a kingly human being ("Presence") for a mere intangible, some future expectation that is "Not now" when the soul craves it. Renunciation blinds the eyes of young lovers just opening in the dawn of their happiness, for their temporal day threatens to overwhelm the creator himself. The Latinate tone and biblical associations of "Progenitor" convey the inexorableness of God's demand.

> Renunciation—is the Choosing
> Against itself—
> Itself to justify
> Unto itself—
>
> . . . . . .

The second stanza begins a new definition, investigating the internal consequences of the rejection rather than the outer conflict of the lover and God. The confusion around the repeated "itself" results from her stringent attempts to make the pronoun convey three different states. First, renunciation causes a person to choose against the self of emotions and desires, the physical self that is selfishness. This choice will allow the total personality, man's body and soul suggested by the second "itself," to be justified or regenerated in the eyes of God. The final "itself" is the soul's moral nature, its spiritual essence, which wills renunciation. The last image (where a "larger function" makes "that Covered Vision—Here" appear smaller) indicates that even faith cannot eradicate the regret occasioned by this loss. The spiritual hope is described most formally as a larger function (echoing the "Expectation" and "Progenitor" of earlier lines) that overpowers the smaller, more desirable "Covered Vision." The fact that this temporal love is associated with sunlight, beauty, and vision indicates its value and the difficulty of renouncing it for a vague, foreboding "function." Throughout, the emotional associations clustered about "Presence" emphasize the poignancy of the loss and bitterness of the denial.

Undoubtedly, Emily Dickinson's finest poem about pain and one of her artistic achievements is "After great pain, a formal feeling comes." Here the soul's numbed response after an enervating shock exemplifies a fundamental law: that pain is an unavoidable aspect of human existence. A carefully modulated structure, interlocking images of ceremony and crystallization, and acute psychological observations present the situation. The overall form of the poem exhibits the disjointed death throes of various parts of the body—the nerves, the heart, and the feet—where the dull instinctive reactions of the entire system gradually subside to a static, frozen immobility. The stages of pain pass from a funereal atmosphere, concentrating on images of ceremony and tombs in stanza one, to the mechanical wooden world of stanza two (where "Quartz contentment" is linked with tombs), and finally to the frozen death of stanza three, where leaden images climax in snow's blank desolation. Stately iambic pentameter, matched by rhyming couplets, opens and closes the poem, underscoring the ceremonial aspects of great pain. As Frank Manley has demonstrated in his analysis of the poem, a crystallization image guides the whole poem. Emily Dickinson describes a person who is alive yet insensible, a living organism frozen in eternal numbness.

> After great pain, a formal feeling comes—
> The Nerves sit ceremonious, like Tombs—
> The stiff Heart questions was it He, that bore,
> And Yesterday, or Centuries before?

The poem's opening statement surprises, for great pain does not bring disorder or hysteria, only a carefully controlled, formal sensation that inspires awe. This formal feeling is immediately expanded by the funeral ritual in the next line. Here the usually active nerves sit decorously as people attending a wake, solemnly surrounding the corpse ("ceremonious" hints at a religious consolation, besides relating to the artificiality of funeral services). The final "tomb" image amplifies this ceremonial aspect to suggest oppression and isolation, besides preparing for the later quartz association. Even the dull grey color of tombstones is soon to be reflected by lead and snow images. The heart is stiff, as if overtaxed and aching after so much grief, but it is also rigidly controlled by this funeral service. The heart questions laboriously and haltingly, trying to link its suffering with that of Christ on the cross. Still, the emphasis on "bore" and the grim observation that the pain's intensity makes Calvary immediately present allow little religious consolation and no relief from pain's viselike hold.

> The Feet, mechanical, go round—
> Of Ground, or Air, or Ought—
>
> . . . .
> A Quartz contentment, like a stone—

The second stanza deepens this despair by picturing the body as a mechanical object, a toy puppet, aimlessly dangling on its strings in a terrible parody of life's vitality. The "o" assonance captures the hollow thud of numbed feet bumping against wooden planking. The image progresses from walking to a helpless swinging in mid-air and finally to a circle of frustrating movement. "Ought" has various implications, the terror of being trapped in an endless circle, the daily round of social obligations and duties, and the ought of zero, the nothingness of blank despair. Finally, a "Quartz contentment" describes the body's state, suggesting quartz's hard, glossy finish as well as its smooth tactile quality that is unpleasantly cold. Yet this is a contentment, since this suspended state signifies the superior rank to which great pain has elevated the soul. Though somewhat like the vegetative life of a stone, this achievement has the more precious, regal qualities associated with quartz.

> This is the Hour of Lead—
> Remembered, if outlived,
> As Freezing persons, recollect the Snow—
> First—Chill—then Stupor—then the letting go—

The final stanza completes the crystallization process. The base, dull color of lead prepares for the image of a person slowly freezing to death in the snow. The final line summarizes the whole poem as this pain progresses from the first sudden chill which retards movement and control to the numbness of wooden motion, until eventually the letting go of death and total inactivity occur. This, then, is the way one experiences pain, by a complete death of the senses and a freezing of all hope and activity. Paradoxically, the poet concludes that the real effect of pain is its absence, the utter numbness that only a severe wound could physically produce.

Certainly one of Emily Dickinson's unique contributions to American literature is her poetic insight into the nature of death. Closely related to her knowledge of pain and longing for eternal life, this understanding of death was demonstrated in more than five hundred lyrics.

The range of her poetic treatment varied from a philosophical examination of death's relation with love to a grim consideration of its physical processes. As she surveyed the broad universe and society itself, Emily Dickinson perceived that death remained the one free agent, greater than nature and second only to God. She considered death the great unknown and never ceased to ponder its fascination and mystery. If death resulted in despair and terror, it also brought rest and peace and increased one's enjoyment of life. Death came as a wily courtier, stealthily wooing with a counterfeit charm. It commanded one's presence as a king, stung like an insect, maneuvered like a snake, visited as an old friend, ruthlessly killed as a hired assassin—the images are endless, furnishing a complete natural history of death. In fact, Emily Dickinson once wrote a mock biographical sketch of death, "Dust is the only Secret," noting that death was the only one who remained unknown in his home town. In the role of a reporter bewildered by the elusive facts, she remarks that his parents were unknown and that he grew up without play-mates. This poem typifies many of her verses that personify death, of which "Because I could not stop for Death" is the finest. She closely examined the sensations of the dying, the response of the on-lookers, the terrible struggle of the body for life, the adjustments in a house after death, the arranging of the body for the funeral, the church services, and even the thoughts of the dead person. In her best poems she minimized death's sensational and emotional aspects to plumb its ultimate relation with love and immortality and to sound the reaches of its frightening power.

Still, she wrote many inferior lyrics on death, which were filled with bathos, sentimentality, and morbidness. Like the worst of the Gift Book versifiers, she often imagined herself dead with mourners filing by, or dying in order to punish indifferent friends. At times these poems reflect Emmeline Grangerford's mawkish production of deathbed lyrics so superbly satirized in *Huckleberry Finn*. Still, in her finest poems like "She lay as if at play" she transformed these platitudes into enduring poetry.

Some of her best lyrics on death considered the sensations of the dying person, the physical experiences as the soul leaves the body. In all these poems tension is established by contrasting the inertness of the dead person with the movement of the living and the external growth of nature. "I heard a Fly buzz—when I died" contrasts the expectations of death with its realistic occurrence. The traditional Christian belief that death leads to eternal happiness is undercut by the appearance of an insignificant, distracting fly.

I heard a Fly buzz—when I died—
The Stillness in the Room
Was like the Stillness in the Air
Between the Heaves of Storm—

The Eyes around—had wrung them dry—
And Breaths were gathering firm
For that last Onset—when the King
Be witnessed—in the Room—

The opening lines jolt as the buzz of a fly ludicrously interrupts the awesome approach of death. After this initial shock the poet describes the atmosphere of the sick room. The moment is tense; the soul is poised, ready to depart; and the stillness in the room is like the deceptively calm center of a hurricane. The second stanza considers the dry-eyed and expectant onlookers, as they crowd closer to view the last dying movements. The scene appears morbid to modern readers; yet it was common practice in Emily Dickinson's time to observe the dying. For those with a religious faith, the moment of death meant that a soul left its body to enter paradise. Thus the dying person's final actions were carefully scrutinized for an indication of immortality's approach. Even Emily Dickinson avidly hoped that the last words or gestures before death would ease some of her own doubts about immortality. The final death struggle of soul and body is termed an "Onset," as the king sweeps majestically in with the treasures of paradise. Like disciples giving testimony to the grandeur of God, the onlookers expect to witness this sublime ceremony.

The last two stanzas bring the climax:

I willed my Keepsakes—Signed away
. . . .
. . . and then it was
There interposed a Fly—

With Blue—uncertain stumbling Buzz—
Between the light—and me—
And then the Windows failed—and then
I could not see to see—

The final acts of the dying person are presented with a crisp detachment. In its careful preparation for Death's entrance, the soul rigidly controls the final moments. The pun in "Signed" and "Assignable" ironically illustrates death's supreme power, for only worthless documents, empty phrases, curious mementos, and a corrupting body can be left behind. The irony increases as the soul precisely arranges everything and waits confidently for death. Now the grand moment is at hand, but unfortunately a fly interrupts the ceremony.

Like so much of life's experience the fly comes at the wrong time, as a petty irritant which distracts from the magnificent approach of death. What the dying person fails to realize is that the fly signalizes death's presence. Its stumbling blue buzz, an apt synesthetic image that conveys the confusion of the dying mind, imitates the pattern of life, where moments of beauty and confidence are juxtaposed with ugliness and uncertainty. The fly comes between the light and the dying person, not just blocking physical sight but obscuring the radiance of immortality as well. The final line captures the desperate intensity of the person's struggle for life. Instead of the calm assurance of the earlier stanzas, the person now fails to recognize death's arrival and fights to prevent subjection. Pathetically the person claims that the windows fail, not his eyesight. "I could not see to see" is the last effort at self-control. In these few seconds the soul says that it could not will its eyes open for a final view. One of the deepest ironies here is the soul's confidence that it still controls the body. Only the reader knows the hopelessness of these attempts and how aptly the fly symbolizes life and death, since its buzz is associated with daily household activities, while its food often consists of carrion. The whole poem satirizes the traditional view of death as a peaceful release from life's pressures and a glorious entrance into immortality. Emily Dickinson sees only disappointment, a buzzing fly, and the terrible attempts of a soul to prolong life.

A more disturbing portrayal of death is "I felt a Funeral, in my Brain." With its detailed presentation of a complete funeral as felt through the ebbing sensations of a dead person, this poem borders on the morbid in portraying the terrible struggle that the separation of the body from the soul occasions. Here is no hope of immortality, only a despairing plunge into an eternal abyss. Still, as many critics have noted, the funeral service is not merely exploited for sensational effects, but it has an allegorical significance. The physical death symbolizes spiritual decease and perhaps a momentary insight into the nature of infinity. The opening stanza sets the tone of the poem:

> I felt a Funeral, in my Brain,
> And Mourners to and fro
> Kept treading—treading—till it seemed
> That Sense was breaking through—

The scene opens with the mourners filing past the exposed body before the actual funeral service begins. The atmosphere is oppressive and the incessant pounding of muffled feet seems physically to torment the brain. In the next stanza the mourners are seated and the funeral begins. The formality of this ceremony penetrates the soul like throbbing drums to induce a drugged weariness. In stanza three, bolts of lead trample across her soul as the coffin is closed and carried outside the church. "Then Space—began to toll" and the bells sounding in the background temporarily thrust her into infinity.

> As all the Heavens were a Bell,
> And Being, but an Ear,
> And I, and Silence, some strange Race
> Wrecked, solitary, here—
>
> And then a Plank in Reason, broke,
> And I dropped down, and down—
> And hit a World, at every plunge,
> And Finished knowing—then—

The tension increases as the body is carried to the grave. The bells obliterate all other sensations, casting the soul upon eternity itself, but without hope of resurrection. Reeling under these continual blows, the soul experiences complete disintegration with the tumbling of the casket into the grave. "Finished knowing" completes the loss of conscious control as the soul swirls into the irrational unknown, into an indifferent universe.

The emphasis on dying sensations and failing powers suggests death's dreadful isolation. On another level the initial phrase "in my Brain" hints that this physical death represents some terrible emotional pain or loss that brings an overwhelming sense of despair. Since the soul has lost its reason for living, the person ceases to exist. In an original interpretation of the poem, George Monteiro holds that it deals with the direct knowledge of the absolute when the soul gains a temporary insight into the infinite. Death symbolizes this, since it is one of the few crucial experiences that reveals a glimpse of final things. Monteiro concludes that the poem combines both triumph and failure, for man must return to reality after breaking through the barriers of sense into infinity.

In another large themal grouping, the poet allows a detached observer to view death and analyze its effects upon the dying person. "I've seen a Dying Eye" captures the feverish intensity of a dying person's search for a "Something," which is found without ever being disclosed to the intent onlooker. Thus death continues to baffle all human efforts to comprehend its meaning. Another poem, "How many times these low feet staggered," explores the terrible physical transformation caused by death. Only images of iron and stone recall this once vital soul. Yet, in the final stanza death brings a release from pain and guilt and frees one from the monotonous toil of sewing and dusting. This poem achieves a subtle characterization of the dead woman, gaining our sympathy while baffling our understanding. One of the best poems in this group is "The last Night that She lived." Unlike its presentation in "I heard a Fly buzz—when I died," death is here envisioned as a graceful departure into the sublime waters of immortality. Pain and loss recede as the dead woman obtains eternal peace. The opening stanzas quietly contrast the movement of the onlookers with the tranquillity of death's presence. Death's piercing light illuminates important things, besides radiating grace and salvation. The middle stanzas present the mixed responses of the dead woman's friends. They are grieved that she must die while others less worthy still live; yet they resent her escape into infinity when they must endure more of life's pain. The next stanzas describe her death with the beautiful image of a slender, fragile reed gently bent by the winds. The reed shudders momentarily as it touches the cold waters of eternity, then, as if in glad response, consents to go with death. The final stanza conveys the depression following death as the living busy themselves with funeral arrangements and wait to face the endless pain of time's separation. Even the hope that their religious belief will control this pain is tinged with irony, for emotions cannot be so confidently ordered. The finality of death leaves one helpless and even shakes faith's consolation.

Some of Emily Dickinson's "observer" poems on death emphasize its physical aspects to illustrate the terrible emptiness occasioned by the soul's departure. In "Too cold is this" she portrays death's complete dominion over life with chilling detachment.

> Too cold is this
> To warm with Sun—
> Too stiff to bended be,
>
> . . . .
>
> How went the Agile Kernel out
> Contusion of the Husk
> Nor Rip, nor wrinkle indicate
> But just an Asterisk.

Images of coldness and stone contrast the body's former vitality with its present immobility. As a slab of polished marble that merely glistens in the sun, the body is so inflexible that even the finest craftsman could not "joint" its pieces. Unlike the God of the Old

Testament whom Ezekiel described resurrecting the dry bones in the valley, this master mason cannot revitalize this inert, blankly staring mass. The second stanza considers how the life principle was extinguished, contrasting nature's cycle of death and rebirth with man's departure into the infinite unknown. The mystery of the soul's exit is heightened, since the usual signs attendant upon such a loss are missing. There is no contusion or rip, only a blank asterisk, the typed symbol placed beside a person's name to indicate his death. The impersonality and callousness of the image manifest the desolation of the body once the soul has fled.

A fuller examination of death that deepens its philosophical and religious implications is "A Clock stopped." Using the superstition of a clock stopping when a person dies and the age-old comparison of life to a timepiece, she portrays death as the sudden breakdown of a carefully constructed Swiss clock. At noon its intricately carved figurine bows to announce the hour and then remains there dangling as the long pendulum below is stilled. The shift from movement to immobility comes with frightening haste as death plunges this clock mechanism into a soundless, snowy isolation. The grim comparison of man to a mechanical device emphasizes his meaninglessness. Instead of a glorious immortality the soul is faced with a fearful strangeness once it leaves the body. The faint suggestion of immortality in "Degreeless Noon" and the arrogance of the "Him" (the soul) after leaving the body offer slim consolation, a most qualified view of resurrection that runs counter to orthodox belief. The structure of the poem balances the first two stanzas, which deal with the physical aspects of the body at death, against the last two stanzas, which consider the futile efforts of the doctor and the new arrogance of the soul now freed from its trinket body.

> A Clock stopped—
> Not the Mantel's—
> Geneva's farthest skill
> Cant put the puppet bowing—
> That just now dangled still—
>
> An awe came on the Trinket!
> The Figures hunched, with pain—
> Then quivered out of Decimals—
> Into Degreeless Noon—

The halving of the first line emphasizes that this cessation signifies more than the mere breakdown of a mantel clock. The Swiss clock metaphor controls the whole poem. Geneva was, of course, a center for the watchmaking industry and also the residence of John Calvin, a great designer of Protestantism's complex philosophy. But even this master craftsman cannot repair the unwound springs and broken gears of this clock life. The image of the bowing figurine, suspended in a parody of human courtesy, suggests man's robot life, which is rigidly controlled by a puppet master. Ironically, even his power is ineffective. In the second stanza "awe" hardly fits a cheap trinket, and this incongruity mocks the hope that the figure might have envisioned God before its death. The next lines focus on the moment of death, the dying throes of the puppet. The pun in "Figures" is related to the whole clock concept and expanded in "quivered out of Decimals." No more seconds can be counted off, for the hands of the clock are superimposed on noon. Though hardly a comforting metaphor for immortality, "Degreeless Noon" represents the timelessness of eternity, the moment when the clock completes its cycle and the sun is brightest. Death brings little glory and less assurance.

> . . . .
> The Shopman importunes it—
> While cool—concernless No—
>
> Nods from the Gilded pointers—
> Nods from the Seconds slim—
> Decades of Arrogance between
> The Dial life—
> And Him—

The next two stanzas shift to the harried efforts of the designer-doctor to restore life. His failure blasphemously hints at limitations in God's power. He can create, but indifference and cold arrogance mock his pitiful efforts at restoration. The life force itself ("Pendulum") is frozen and white and suggests negation and despair with its repeated "No." Still, a touch of solemnity enters as death bestows new dignity. The entrance into eternity puts decades of difference between meaningless "Dial life," a physical existence guided by Calvinism's legal-religious sanctions, and the new existence in eternity. The poem concludes as it began, with a halved line, emphasizing the personal pronoun "Him." This cannot refer to the neuter trinket corpse or to the shopman who still resides in a temporal dial life, but only to the soul that leaves once the body dies. Thus the previous hints of immortality in "awe" and "Degreeless Noon" receive full expansion. The whole poem subtly blends the despairing reality of physical death and the frightening limitations of temporal life with the mystery of eternity. Though death ends physical life, it does not cause complete loss, but only a change and separation that baffle the onlookers. The bitter tone is mitigated by the suggestion of the soul's existence after death. The poem might be read as a satire of Calvinism's precise and logical philosophy, which codifies man's life only to break down when faced with the reality of death, and in this sense it is reminiscent of Oliver Wendell Holmes's "The Deacon's Masterpiece," with its witty satire of the disintegration of Calvinism's "one-hoss shay."

Emily Dickinson's numerous elegies form a coda to her examination of death. Especially in her later years elegies constituted many of her poems. An earlier one, "More Life—went out—when He went," eulogizes the vital personality and spiritual force that made this man so superior to other common lives and so difficult for death to subdue. Also, her quatrains on her nephew Gilbert's death capture the innocence of his young soul. Appropriately, her finest elegy was written about her father. For years after his death she continued to mourn his loss and refer to him in letters. In 1877 she wrote to Higginson: "Since my Father's dying, everything sacred enlarged so—it was dim to own" and goes on speaking about the church's view of immortality. Suddenly she asks if Higginson had any doubts himself, remarks that she had been rereading his poem "Decoration," and gives her poem:

> Lay this Laurel on the One
> Too intrinsic for Renown—
> Laurel—veil your deathless tree—
> Him you chasten . . .

Higginson's poem conventionally wonders what tribute best honors the courage of dead soldiers. A mourner goes with flowers for the "bravest of the brave," but decides instead to pay tribute to a mother's untended grave, for the greatest valor is unseen and unacknowledged. What took Higginson twenty-eight lines she condensed into four and captured, as Higginson later admitted, the finer essence of the thought.

The poem directly addresses the mourner to lay his laurel, the traditional symbol of victory and an evergreen plant associated with the metamorphosis of forms, on the "One." The capitalization underscores his distinct individuality. The second line expands this by saying that the inner values that made him superior were too much a part of his very essence to obtain external renown. His virtues were even more singular, since they were not displayed for others to see. The tone shifts in the next two lines as the poet commands the laurel to veil its conventional sign ("deathless tree"), since no external symbol can capture the greatness of this man. In one sense such a display would "chasten" or punish the man, for he would never attach any significance to the tribute. Another reading for the line, using "chasten" as "subdued" or "conquered," might be that, despite his great qualities, he is but a mortal man. So the poet asks nature to mourn for his death by temporarily covering its laurel, whose deathless evergreen mocks man's frail mortality. One further reading, using "chasten" as "refining" or "purifying," enlarges the concept of superiority in "One" to indicate that he has not been destroyed, only changed to something finer. Since his soul lives in paradise, nature's deathless quality has been transcended.

The profound implications in this small lyric show Emily Dickinson's skill in enriching her considerations of death with philosophical overtones and in deepening conventional themes with original insights. Few America poets analyzed death with such variety and intensity. True to her own soul, she never flinched from death's harsh reality nor ever ceased considering the various ways she might face this supreme adversary. Significantly one of her last poems is entitled, "So give me back to Death."

8

IMMORTALITY

In the midst of her most creative years Emily Dickinson wrote:

> The Only News I know
> Is Bulletins all Day
> From Immortality.
>
> . . . .
>
> The Only One I meet
> Is God—The Only Street—
> Existence—This traversed

She never wrote truer lines, for the sublime light of immortality illuminated all areas of her poetic interests. With her Calvinistic rearing and religious bent of mind, such a preoccupation with death and immortality was not unnatural. Her letters and poems continually referred to the problems of faith, the identity of the soul, and the reality of God. Even before writing poetry, she considered these themes, remarking in an early letter: "To live, and die, and mount again in triumphant body, and *next* time, try the upper air—is no schoolboy's theme!" She told Higginson that immortality was the "Flood subject" and then cryptically added: "Paradise is of the option. Whosoever will Own in Eden notwithstanding Adam and Repeal." She pleaded for religious assurance, and with the losses of Newton, her father, Bowles, Wadsworth, and Lord she questioned if immortality were true. Immortality's unknown expanse excited her inquiring mind, while her perplexity with its mystery became a strategy for achieving poetic tension. Almost any aspect of doubt and belief can be found in her writings on immortality; she desired personal immortality and asserted that the soul never changed; yet, she denied the orthodox vision of paradise and even feared that eternity would be cosmic annihilation. Still, throughout her writings certain basic motifs appear. While she felt that the very intensity and significance of human existence forecast its continuance after death, she continually wondered if paradise could ever surpass earthly beauty or human love. Her confidence that love endured beyond the grave bulwarked her hopes for immortality. Her poems associate love, eternity, beauty, God, and even circumference with immortality. Though never certain that death was the threshold of immortality, she firmly believed that the soul's identity could not be lost.

Closely related to her poems on immortality are those on orthodox subjects like the Trinity and the doctrine of the Last Judgment, and such broader philosophic issues as the relation of heaven to earth and the identity of the soul. "I know that He exists" typifies her approach to religious subjects. The initial assumption of faith is qualified by the rest of the poem, until only doubt and an unorthodox position remain. She knows that God's elusiveness is merely a pose which will increase our happiness in immortality. Yet, immediately she wonders if this game of hide-and-seek could be in earnest. Though a few other poems enlarge this hint of dispair, the majority accept God as a true personality whom she could love, hate, joke with, and be irritated by. As Thomas H. Johnson has noted: "It was the very intimacy which she felt for the person of God that enabled her to engage in such banter." Mainly she accepted God as the omnipotent ruler and respected the supreme majesty of his person. Despite her wavering and doubts, she retained her personal faith.

One large area in her religious poetry considered the relation of human love and experiences to life in paradise. Even God himself, she felt, was dependent on human love for complete happiness. One of her poems on the connection of heaven and earth, "I never felt at Home—Below," whimsically states that she doubts if heaven will please her, since only saints will be there. Finally she remarks that only the fear of Judgment Day prevents her running away. Certainly her best poems about religion wittily comment on conventional piety and orthodox beliefs. "Some keep the Sabbath going to Church" mocks the weekly churchgoers for making their religion a Sunday affair. Another poem burlesques the historical significance of the Bible and ridicules the orthodox insistence on doom and damnation:

> The Bible is an antique Volume—
> Written by faded Men
> At the suggestion of Holy Spectres—

Here "antique" connotes something outdated and impractical, rather than rare or precious. Like other old history books, the Bible was not written by inspired prophets, but by "faded Men" who have paled with the passing of centuries. Rather than divine inspiration, the weak urgings of specters prompted their chronicle. Here the entire concept of the Bible's truth and sacredness is reduced to the level of ghost tales and implausible invention. In pedagogical fashion the poem continues, listing the Bible's subjects, Bethlehem and Eden; its main actors, Satan, Judas, and David; and its central concern, the "distinguished Precipice" of sin. Applying these concepts to conventional religion, she notes that boys who believe are very "lonesome," while other boys are "lost." The poem concludes:

> Had but the Tale a warbling Teller—
> All the Boys would come—
> Orpheus' Sermon captivated—
> It did not condemn—

Another poem dealing with the Last Judgment accepts the orthodox view but individualizes it with her personal concept of circumference. The wry blend of humor and disbelief that opens the poem soon changes into a complete and solemn acceptance.

> No Crowd that has occurred
> Exhibit—I suppose
> That General Attendance
> That Resurrection—does—
>
> Circumference be full—
> The long restricted Grave
> Assert her Vital Privilege—
> The Dust—connect—and live—

At the Last Judgment the final transcending of human bonds occurs as the resurrected body rejoins the soul to await its individual sentence. The poem concludes that nothing in life can equal the significance of this moment.

Her fascination with immortality found its most imaginative expression in the poems dealing with circumference, the earthly vision of immortality's haunting reality. In "I taste a liquor never brewed" a drinking conceit describes the ecstasy that accompanies a revelation. The exaggerated phrases convey the divine exhilaration of this insight. A more finished philosophic statement of this vision, "The Soul's Superior instants," employs images of regality and elusiveness to describe the moment. Original metaphors capture the paradoxical theme: that the most significant experience in life remains the most intangible and fleeting. The poem concludes that only a few ever perceive the vision of immortality. Her most searching examination of the unusual effects of grace upon the human soul is "The farthest

Thunder that I heard." The principal metaphor that describes an electric storm clearing the air on a hot, humid day suggests the spiritual explosion that occurs when divine grace comes. As a visible sign of a sacramental experience, this bolt of lightning eternally marks her soul.

> Indebtedness to Oxygen
> The Happy may repay,
> But not the obligation
> To Electricity—
> It founds the Homes and decks the Days
> And every clamor bright
> Is but the gleam concomitant
> Of that waylaying Light—

Since oxygen is a basic element in supporting human life, the dependent living can acknowledge their debt to it. However, this "Electricity" is a hidden, mysterious force that baffles understanding and demands humble acceptance. It forms the basis for spiritual growth and adorns life with beauty and faith.

Her finest poem on the philosophic implications of this vision, one that relates immortality and death, is "Behind Me—dips Eternity." The poem focuses on the moment of death as the soul hovers between chaos and eternity. The apocalyptic theme is presented with solemnity and grandeur, soaring and expanding to the farthest reaches of the poetic imagination. Unlike some of her other lyric expressions, this poem is ordered by a consistent philosophic view and a carefully wrought structure. Somewhat like Wordsworth's "Ode: Intimations of Immortality from Recollections of Early Childhood," the poem views human existence as a brief term, surrounded by the expanse of God, and pictures the soul as pre-existing in eternity and returning there after death. However, the religious conviction is qualified by the fear that it may not be true. Controlled by a light-dark metaphor, the poem has a threefold structure. It moves from the present confidence of a soul standing at the threshold of eternity to a vision of paradise, with its perfect bliss in the second stanza, until the third stanza suggests the underlying doubt and terror of the moment. The basic images contrast the light of the dawn and the moon against the darkness of death and despair, and an insistent repetition of key words, a heavily accentuated rhetorical pattern, and a striking alliteration of "d," "m," and "b" sounds convey the solemnity of the experience.

> Behind Me—dips Eternity—
> Before Me—Immortality—
> Myself—The Term between—
> Death but the Drift of Eastern Gray,
> Dissolving into Dawn away,
> Before the West begin—

The first stanza opens with the soul facing east in total isolation. Behind her is the setting sun and twilight; but, just as the sun only seems to disappear before man's limited sight, so the divine presence ("Eternity") remains even in death. Before her is the hope of dawn ("Immortality"), an assuring proof of a new life. As Charles Anderson notes: "Her gaze is for the moment so fixed on these two radiant zones she has no words for the mortal existence she actually knows." So she calls life a "Term," something short and limited, which suggests a term of prison confinement. Death itself is only a passing gray cloud that dissolves before the dawn of Immortality.

> 'Tis Kingdoms—afterward—they say—
> In perfect—pauseless Monarchy—
> Whose Prince—is Son of None—
> Himself—His Dateless Dynasty—
> Himself—Himself diversify—
> In Duplicate divine—

The vision is introduced with a qualified "they say," as if she has to strengthen her belief by quoting the proper authorities. Though the soul feels this sense of the Divine, it cannot be certain, and the doubt suggested here is to be expanded in the last stanza. However, the view of heaven's prince is awesome and filled with traditional reverence for the mystery of the Godhead. The hushed mood captures the splendor and perfect peace of immortality. Though Christ is surprisingly called the "Son of None" instead of the "Son of Man," the title aptly suggests Christ's lack of a human father and his timeless existence. The triple "Himself" hints at the mystery of the Trinity, while God's re-creation of himself in "Duplicate Divine" echoes the statement in Genesis about man's being made in God's image and likeness.

> . . . .
> A Crescent in the Sea—
> With Midnight to the North of Her—
> And Midnight to the South of Her—
> And Maelstrom—in the Sky—

As a perfect coda, the third stanza repeats the initial pattern, admitting that immortality is a miracle, unexplainable by reason or science. Life now appears as a crescent, a slender moon which rises out of the raging black waters. As a mere reflection the moon is utterly dependent on the sun's light, and this image parallels the "Duplicate Divine" concept, while also indicating the world of flux and change in which man exists. The final lines present the alternative to this faith in immortality—the terror of midnight and the destructive power of a maelstrom. So the poem ends with the evocative image of the fragile moon just evading annihilation. The slender thread of faith is stretched to near breaking, but the triumphant vision of the "perfect—pauseless Monarchy" seems secure at last.

Emily Dickinson's most typical approach to the problem of immortality is seen in "This World is not Conclusion." After a definite assertion of belief, the poem explores the perplexing inability of philosophers, scholars, and saints to prove adequately the truth of immortality.

> This World is not Conclusion.
> A Species stands beyond—
> Invisible, as Music—
> But positive, as Sound—

Even the opening lines are double-edged. After the firm statement of faith her position is qualified by the indefinite term "Species." Her comparison of immortality with music increases the doubt, for invisible and intangible sounds are hardly positive proof. The middle lines follow this pragmatic approach as she finds the testimony of philosophers and martyrs unconvincing. As if writing an autobiography, she remarks:

> Faith slips—and laughs, and rallies—
> Blushes, if any see—
> Plucks at a twig of Evidence—
> And asks a Vane, the way—

Faith, as if a bit intoxicated, wavers in her attempts to follow the righteous paths of the saints. Slipping and falling, she clutches at weak twigs for support and then helplessly asks a weather vane for directions. The final lines satirize the empty gestures and "Strong Hallelujahs" that orthodox religion substitutes for faith and conclude that such religion is like a narcotic that "cannot still the Tooth/ That nibbles at the soul."

"A Solemn thing within the Soul" furnishes another approach to immortality. The traditional image of fruit ripening in the sun reveals the confidence and tranquillity brought by faith. Among Emily Dickinson's examinations of immortality this poem remains unique, since it conveys perfect resignation and serene submission to God's will. Two other poems, "Though the great Waters sleep" and "My Cocoon tightens—Colors tease," also delineate the assurance of immortality. The former employs an original fire-water metaphor that reminds one of Robert Frost's meditation on the world's end in "Fire and Ice."

Emily Dickinson surveyed every area of immortality's domain, examining its relations with death and love, satirizing its solemnity, depicting its terrible isolation, and philosophically probing its effects upon the soul. Her best poems on immortality have another New England trait, a philosophic toughness. "Two Lengths has every Day" logically argues that the identity of the soul cannot be lost in immortality:

> Two Lengths has every Day—
> It's absolute extent
> And Area superior
> By Hope or Horror lent—
>
> Eternity will be
> Velocity or Pause
> At Fundamental Signals
> From Fundamental Laws.

.   .   .   .

The poem examines a common psychological experience, that the soul not only realistically perceives an object but imaginatively creates its full impression. So each day has two lengths, an absolute one of twenty-four hours, which can be accurately measured, and an "Area superior," which depends upon a soul's mood. Arguing from this basic truth, Emily Dickinson says that eternity will be similar, either an active, evolving existence ("Velocity") or a static, suspended state ("Pause"). Since the transitory customs of the earth will be eliminated, eternity's new requirements will be based on the essence of man and God. The final stanza asserts that death will not destroy the soul or even change its identity, for man's individual consciousness will guide his journey to immortality.

Another poem that investigates the mystery of eternity accentuates its strangeness, for terror and alienation replace the assurance of "Two Lengths has every Day." This poem examines the perplexity of a soul accustomed to time-space limitations in adjusting to the new dimensions of infinity.

> Great Streets of silence led away
> To Neighborhoods of Pause—
> Here was no Notice—no Dissent
> No Universe—no Laws—
>
> By Clocks, 'twas Morning, and for Night
> The Bells at Distance . . .
> But Epoch had no basis here
> For Period exhaled.

The introductory image shows how frightening and oppressive familiar streets and neighborhoods become when human activity and sound are removed. Then follows a closer examination of how completely infinity severs all the connecting links with humanity. Eternity has "no Notice," no signs or guides to indicate where one is or where one should go. Nor is any "Dissent" possible here, since God's absolute rule will allow man neither volition nor individuality. Then "no Universe" can be seen, for infinity has no accustomed landmarks, only blankness. Finally, there are "no Laws," since the usual rules that govern normal society will be suspended. These clipped negations suggest the chilling emptiness that a loss of these familiar things occasions.

In the second stanza the strangeness assumes nightmarish proportions as temporal time is completely confused. Clocks indicate morning, while distant bells toll out an evening curfew. After the pause and silence of the first stanza, the reappearance of time and sound should be reassuring, but this discord only increases the fear. The poem stresses the transformation that eternity demands, the adaptation of one's earthly consciousness to a new perspective. At first this appears impossible, but the final lines offer a glimmer of hope. The soul must realize that its former gauges of time and history ("Epoch") have no pertinence here. Yet the final personification, that of time slowly exhaling to wipe out forever dates and facts ("Period"), leaves an appalling vacuum. The poem shows the bewilderment of a soul newly entering paradise and the fear that lies at immortality's core.

Two other lyrics demonstrate the variety and depth of her examination of immortality, in addition to revealing her ambivalent feelings about faith. "Those not live yet" is one of her most confident statements about the existence of the soul after death. Signed

"Easter," the poem triumphantly asserts that death brings no substantial change:

> Those not live yet
> Who doubt to live again—
> "Again" is of a twice
>
> . . . .
> The Ship beneath the Draw
> Aground—is he?
> Death—so—the Hyphen of the Sea—
> Deep is the Schedule
> Of the Disk to be—
> Costumeless Consciousness—
> That is he—

Paradoxically, the poem opens by addressing those who question immortality's truth. These doubters are not actually alive, she says, for without immortality's hope man exists as a dead spirit in a physical body. Yet, the word "again" annoys her and she pauses to clarify its implications. To live again indicates an alteration, a renewal of life, while the immortal soul is essentially one and can undergo no substantial modification. Three disparate images of the ship, the hyphen, and the disk analogously attempt to demonstrate this puzzling truth. The first image portrays a ship beneath the drawbridge, progressing slowly through a narrow channel from one body of water to another. When viewed from the shore, the moving ship appears to be aground. Similarly, the soul in its voyage through the waters of earth to heaven's sea undergoes no essential change. Death itself functions as a connecting link between life and immortality, a hyphen similar to the draw. Expanding this nautical image, the final lines envision eternity itself. The schedule or the itinerary of this ship in its passage to immortality is "deep," since it physically moves beyond terrestrial limits, traveling into the realms of the spirit. The radical shift of the ship image to that of the disk prepares for the last metaphor. The soul in discarding its body becomes a mere outline or disk. Though the substantial soul is there, it lacks the flesh and blood of an individual body and appears as a "Costumeless Consciousness." What is left after this draw-hyphen experience of death is only identity, one's soul stripped of its physical accidents. Joyously she cries, "That is he," the core of one's being. Here the conventional idea of immortality, with its insistence upon splendor and majestic transformation, is uniquely reworked to present her belief in the reality of the soul after death.

Appropriately, the last poem in this section, "Safe in their Ala-

Emily Dickinson*

baster Chambers," stands as one of Emily Dickinson's finest lyrics on the ambiguous relation of death and immortality.[1] Neither the terror of death nor the assurance of immortality are presented here, only a sense of the sublimity and isolation that death imposes. The poem examines various attitudes on death and immortality: first, the consolations of faith and hope in resurrection; then the loss of animation and physical vigor; and finally, the fearful grandeur of the soul's new immortal existence. The key images contrast nature's vitality with the enclosed, alabaster condition of the dead and the slow, stately movement of eternity. From the assurances of conventional faith the poem moves to the enigmatic immortality attainable in the distant expanse of infinity.

> Safe in their Alabaster Chambers—
> Untouched by Morning—
> And untouched by Noon—
> Lie the meek members of the Resurrection—
> Rafter of Satin—and Roof of Stone!
>
> Light laughs the breeze
> In her Castle above them—
> Babbles the Bee in a stolid Ear,
>
> . . . .

A surface reading of this first stanza offers a confident assertion of orthodox resurrection, as the souls serenely await the Last Judgment and reunion with their glorified bodies. However, the adjective "Safe" links these elect to a smug, self-satisfied piousness. Mocked by the bright warmth of the morning and the vibrant sounds and activity of nature, these dead are truly untouched, deprived of life's vitality and denied sensation. Instead, they remain in alabaster perfection, encased in a precious white marble, frightening in its cold, translucent smoothness. Their graves are luxurious, spacious chambers, decorated with rafters of satin; but none of these frills conceal their lifeless, stone existence. Rather, the simple dignity of death shuns such ostentation. The image of the "meek members" openly satirizes the book of Revelation's account of the assembled elect and presents them as timid time-servers, whose goodness resulted from fears of damnation and society's pressures. Even the soft, plushy "m" sounds

[1] Emily Dickinson apparently could not decide on a final form for this poem, inasmuch as it exists in two different versions, one of which was written in 1859 and the other in 1861. Both versions have a similar first stanza and differing second ones. Following the approach used by Charles Anderson, I have combined the two poems to form a three-stanza poem. The 1861 version is followed here except for the second stanza, which comes from the 1859 poem.

reflect this feeling. The singsong final lines suggest that their religious convictions are thin tinsel, a decorative coating which cannot conquer the stone reality of death. The second stanza presents another view of death, its terrible deprivation of physical vitality. Utilizing a series of clichés, the light laughter of the breeze, the babble of the bee, and the piping of the birds, it contrasts nature's careless freedom and idle happiness with the closed solemnity and "sagacity" of these cold dead.

The final approach to immortality bypasses religion's assurances and nature's mindless energy to suggest the actual grandeur of death.

> Grand go the Years—in the Crescent—
> above them—
> Worlds scoop their Arcs—
> And Firmaments—row—
> Diadems—drop—and Doges—surrender—
> Soundless as dots—on a Disc of Snow—

Instead of personal identity or orthodox resurrection, immortality brings a cessation of pain and effort, an entrance into a vast, indifferent universe. The poem moves from the linear, closed images of the tomb into circular, expanding ones of crescents, scoops, and arcs, away from temporal limitations to the grandeur of years and worlds and finally into the firmament itself. The vastness of this eternal cycle dwarfs all other considerations and reveals the insignificance of the waiting meek followers and the childishness of nature's babbling. Eternity disdains temporal time and material existence. The final lines show death's leveling power and portray man's absorption into eternity as the insignificant dropping of a dot on a disc of snow. There is little religious consolation and no acknowledgment of personal immortality, for in death man mingles with nature's white and alien oversoul without personality or sensation. A numbed blankness suggests the superiority, even the majesty, of this ambiguous existence. In her poems on immortality, Emily Dickinson reveals not only her religious depth and preceptive insight into spiritual reality but also her artistic ability in employing both skepticism and faith as a strategy to increase the dramatic tension of her poems. Her final position is best understood by a letter she wrote to Judge Lord near the end of her life: "On subjects of which we know nothing . . . we both believe, and disbelieve a hundred times an Hour, which keeps Believing nimble."

9

ACHIEVEMENT

AMONG OUTSTANDING American writers few had to wait as long for critical and scholarly acceptance as did Emily Dickinson. With just seven poems published in her lifetime, it was not until the 1950s that she was securely placed with Poe and Whitman as a major poet. Such posthumous fame fitted the anonymity of her life and echoed her own prophecy to Higginson: "If fame belonged to me, I could not escape her—if she did not, the longest day would pass me on the chase." Perhaps her unschooled "Barefoot-Rank" better suited her solitary existence than any contemporary fame. Certainly, she carefully maneuvered her withdrawal from Amherst society and tenaciously fought for privacy throughout her life.

Although Transcendentalism's concept of self-reliance satisfied her inquiring spirit more than Calvinism's harsh dogmas, her mind displayed the essential religious texture of the Puritan mentality. Lacking the orthodox confidence in salvation, she employed Puritanism's belief in self-denial to rein her passionate, sensitive nature. Her own suffering taught her that pain and deprivation, rather than happiness, constituted the essence of life. She eschewed the conventional supports of home, society, and religion to fight alone on life's hardest battleground—within the human soul. Unflinchingly she faced inner challenges and struggled to wrest spiritual victory from emotional defeat. Basically she was a religious poet whose concern with the fundamental issues of death, pain, love, and immortality occasioned her finest lyrics. She revitalized the usual poetic approach to God and religion and in her scrupulous record of the soul's "Adventure . . . unto itself" explored new frontiers of sensations and psychological experience. Neither a consistent nor original thinker, she pragmatically tested traditional concepts before accepting their validity. Always analyzing, she sought to tell "all the Truth" and to stun her hearers with the resulting "Bolts of Melody." Like many poets she perceived man as a beleaguered, isolated creature, desperately seeking truth in a relativistic world. Mainly her own thwarted love, unfulfilled poetic ambitions, and dissatisfaction with Calvinism furnished the crude clay from which she molded her finished poems. From her limited, pain-filled experiences she wrung an intense exhilaration with the processes of life. In her poetry she expressed these feelings so originally that the provincial and the private were often translated into enduring, universal art.

Her poetic strategy depended upon the "language of surprise," wit, paradox, and irony, to reveal the naked soul in dramatic conflict with established conventions. Though fascinated by words, she ruthlessly omitted phrases and cut through syntax to achieve conciseness and to capture the spontaneity and excitement of her thoughts. If at times her economy short-circuited full meaning, it also infused her poetry with an electric vibrancy that rivaled the intimacy of the spoken word. As her subjects were limited, so her stylistic traits, aside from her eccentric punctuation, were mainly conventional: hymnal stanzas, repetitious iambics, and a fondness for colloquial expressions and approximate rhyme. Still, her imaginative sense and profound artistic dedication transformed these familiar devices into a lively medium for her thoughts. Of course, critics have extensively catalogued her glaring failures: rampant sentimentality, an excessive preoccupation with death and pain, awkward inversions, monotonous metrics, and an over-all inability to control her exploding poetic force. Yet, measured against the vitality and imaginative scope of her verses, these objections become mere cavils. One gauge of her achievement was the popular appreciation of her poetry long before academicians considered her verse acceptable. Only Robert Frost has had a similar popular and critical success.

Undoubtedly, the areas of life and nature that most interested her were narrow and personal. Still, she probed these subjects deeply and produced a surprising variety of insights about external nature, the inner struggles of the human soul, and the mysteries of death and immortality. Though her nature poems often deal with the pictorial aspects of flowers and sunsets, her most original ones, like "A Route of Evanescence," touch upon the strangeness and elusiveness of nature's "haunted house." "These are the days when Birds come back" and "A Light exists in Spring" imbue the material scene with distinctive religious and regal imagery to sound philosophic overtones. Repeatedly she observed the change of seasons and moments of storm and chose nature's odd creatures to enliven the conventional romantic view of nature. "Of Bronze—and Blaze" utilizes the solemn grandeur of the universe to evoke hauntingly man's frail mortality, while "Further in Summer than the Birds" employs the pensive rituals of a dying year to demonstrate man's alienation from nature.

Another major poetic grouping records an overwhelming passion that progresses to a climactic meeting of the lovers, only to collapse into despairing separation. Even the tensions of physical attraction were frankly handled in poems like "My Life had stood—a Loaded Gun," while another group of poems longingly surveys a wife's estate in marriage. The anxiety of denial and loss provided the framework for intense psychological analyses that gradually brought spiritual consolation. Her sublimation of passion into a religious triumph originated some of her most moving love lyrics, for example, "Title divine—is mine" and "Mine—by the Right of White Election." Continually her poems affirm the value of renunciation, minutely scrutinizing the spiritual good that emerged from such rejection. Like Hawthorne she praised heroism in defeat and carefully examined the educative nature of pain. Many poems commend the stoic courage of those who silently endure their "Calvary of Wo." "Renunciation—is a piercing Virtue" analyzes both the poignancy and bitterness of denial, and "After great pain, a formal feeling comes" portrays the soul's numbed response to an enervating shock.

However, her most searching explorations within the human spirit dealt with death and immortality. She portrayed death from every possible aspect: as the courtly lover, the dreadful assassin, the physical corrupter, and the one free agent in nature. For her, death remained the supreme experience, which brought either new spiritual existence or lifeless immobility. "Because I could not stop for Death," "I Heard a Fly buzz—when I died," and "A Clock stopped" view death's inexorable power, highlighting the physical transformation and chilling isolation that it causes. Often she contrasted the pious expectations of death with its grim reality, employing funereal and religious imagery to dramatize death's approach. Although she interchanged the terms "death" and "immortality," she usually envisioned death as the threshold of that new state. The "Flood subject" of immortality both baffled and intrigued her, and the resulting tensions produced "Behind Me—dips Eternity" and "Safe in their Alabaster Chambers." Though one later poem, "Those not live yet," triumphantly asserts that death brings no change to the immortal soul, she never ceased questioning or anatomizing those ultimates. Reading through her collected poems, one is startled afresh by man's infinite capacity to endure and master suffering.

She once expressed the extent of her achievement:

> The Poets light but Lamps—
> Themselves—go out—

> The Wicks they stimulate—
> If vital Light
>
> Inhere as do the Suns—
> . . . .
> Disseminating their
> Circumference—

Certainly the vital light of genius illuminates her poems. With each succeeding generation they have shone brighter, disseminating their radiant vision of circumference with increasing power and beauty.

SELECTED BIBLIOGRAPHY

EDITIONS OF EMILY DICKINSON'S POEMS

Poems by Emily Dickinson, eds. Mabel Loomis Todd and T. W. Higginson. Boston: Roberts Brothers, 1890.

Poems by Emily Dickinson, Second Series, eds. T. W. Higginson and Mabel Loomis Todd. Boston: Roberts Brothers, 1891.

Poems by Emily Dickinson, Third Series, ed. Mabel Loomis Todd. Boston: Roberts Brothers, 1896.

The Single Hound, ed. Martha Dickinson Bianchi. Boston: Little, Brown & Company, 1914.

The Poems of Emily Dickinson, eds. Martha Dickinson Bianchi and Alfred L. Hampson. Boston: Little, Brown & Company, 1937.

Bolts of Melody, eds. Mabel Loomis Todd and Millicent Todd Bingham. New York: Harper & Row Publishers, 1945.

The Poems of Emily Dickinson, Including Variant Readings Critically Compared with All Known Manuscripts, ed. Thomas H. Johnson. 3 vols. Cambridge: Harvard University Press, 1955. [The definitive edition which finally established the text of the poems. A single volume edition, *The Complete Poems of Emily Dickinson,* and a paperbound selection of the poems, *Final Harvest,* have also been published by Thomas H. Johnson.]

LETTERS

Letters of Emily Dickinson, ed. Mabel Loomis Todd. 2 vols. Boston: Roberts Brothers, 1894.

Letters of Emily Dickinson, ed. Mabel Loomis Todd. New York: Harper & Row Publishers, 1931.

Emily Dickinson's Letters to Dr. and Mrs. Josiah Gilbert Holland, ed. Theodora Ward. Cambridge, Mass.: Harvard University Press, 1951.

Emily Dickinson: A Revelation, by Millicent Todd Bingham. New York: Harper & Row Publishers, 1954.

Emily Dickinson's Home: Letters of Edward Dickinson and His Family, by Millicent Todd Bingham. New York: Harper & Row Publishers, 1955.

The Letters of Emily Dickinson, ed. Thomas H. Johnson. 3 vols. Cambridge, Mass.: Harvard University Press, 1958. [The definitive edition.]

The Lyman Letters: New Light on Emily Dickinson and Her Family, by Richard B. Sewall. Amherst, Mass.: University of Massachusetts Press, 1965.

BIBLIOGRAPHY

Emily Dickinson: . . . A Bibliography, compiled by the Jones Library. Amherst, Massachusetts, 1930.

Rosenbaum, S. P., ed. *A Concordance to the Poems of Emily Dickenson.* Ithaca, N.Y.: Cornell University Press, 1964.

Spiller, Robert E. et al. *Literary History of the United States,* Vol. 3, *Bibliography.* New York: The Macmillan Company, 1948. *Supplement,* ed. Richard Ludwig. New York: The Macmillan Company, 1959.

BIOGRAPHY

Bianchi, Martha Dickinson. *The Life and Letters of Emily Dickinson.* Boston: Houghton Mifflin Company, 1924.

————. *Emily Dickinson Face to Face.* Boston: Houghton Mifflin Company, 1932.

Bingham, Millicent Todd. *Ancestor's Brocades: The Literary Debut of Emily Dickinson.* New York: Harper & Row Publishers, 1945.

Leyda, Jay. *The Years and Hours of Emily Dickinson.* 2 vols. New Haven, Conn.: Yale University Press, 1960. [A valuable documentary record of Emily Dickinson's life, chronologically arranged.]

Patterson, Rebecca. *The Riddle of Emily Dickinson.* Boston: Houghton Mifflin Company, 1951.

Pollitt, Josephine. *Emily Dickinson: The Human Background of Her Poetry.* New York: Harper & Row Publishers, 1930.

Taggard, Genevieve. *The Life and Mind of Emily Dickinson.* New York: Alfred A. Knopf, Inc., 1930.

Ward, Theodora. *The Capsule of the Mind: Chapters in the Life of Emily Dickinson*. Cambridge, Mass.: Harvard University Press, 1961. [A most perceptive study of Emily Dickinson's personality.]

CRITICAL AND INTERPRETATIVE STUDIES

Anderson, Charles H. *Emily Dickinson's Poetry: Stairway of Surprise*. New York: Holt, Rinehart and Winston, Inc., 1960. [A revealing, detailed analysis of Dickinson's main poems and an incisive examination of her poetic theory and manner of writing. By far the finest critical book on Emily Dickinson.]

Chase, Richard. *Emily Dickinson*. New York: William Sloane Associates, 1951.

Gelpi, Albert J. *Emily Dickinson: The Mind of the Poet*. Cambridge, Mass.: Harvard University Press, 1965. [A valuable study of Dickinson's mind.]

Griffith, Clark. *The Long Shadow: Emily Dickinson's Tragic Poetry*. Princeton, N.J.: Princeton University Press, 1964.

Johnson, Thomas H. *Emily Dickinson: An Interpretative Biography*. Cambridge, Mass.: Harvard University Press, 1955. [One of the best balanced of recent biographical and interpretative studies.]

MacLeish, Archibald, Louise Bogan, and Richard Wilbur. *Emily Dickinson: Three Views*. Amherst, Mass.: Amherst College Press, 1960.

Marcus, Mordecai. "Nature Symbolism in the Poetry of Emily Dickinson," unpublished dissertation, University of Kansas, 1958.

Wells, Henry W. *Introduction to Emily Dickinson*. New York: Hendricks House, 1947.

Whicher, George F. *This Was a Poet: A Critical Biography of Emily Dickinson*. New York: Charles Scribner's Sons, 1938. [Though somewhat outdated, this book still remains one of the best accounts of Emily Dickinson's life and writings.]

CRITICAL ARTICLES AND ESSAYS

Aiken, Conrad. "Emily Dickinson," *Dial*, 76 (1924).

Arms, George. "Dickinson's *These Are The Days When Birds Come Back*," *Explicator*, 2 (1944).

Blackmur, Richard P. "Emily Dickinson: Notes on Prejudice and Fact," *The Southern Review*, 3 (1937).

Frye, Northrop. "Emily Dickinson," *Major Writers of America*. Vol. 2. New York: Harcourt, Brace & World, Inc., 1962. [A good short introduction to Dickinson's poetry.]

Higginson, Thomas Wentworth. "Emily Dickinson's Letters," *Atlantic Monthly*, 68 (1891). [An important early essay.]

Manley, Francis. "An Explication of Dickinson's 'After Great Pain,' " *Modern Language Notes*, 73 (1958).

Monteiro, George. "Traditional Ideas in Dickinson's 'I Felt a Funeral in My Brain,' " *Modern Language Notes*, 75 (1960).

Mathiessen, F. O. "The Problem of the Private Poet," *Kenyon Review*, 7 (1945).

Ransom, John Crowe. "Emily Dickinson," *Perspectives USA*, No. 15 (1956).

Scott, Winfield Townley. "Emily Dickinson and Samuel Bowles," *Exiles and Fabrications*. New York: Doubleday & Company, Inc., 1961.

Stamm, Edith P. "Emily Dickinson: Poetry and Punctuation," *Saturday Review*, 46 (1963).

Tate, Allen. "New England Culture and Emily Dickinson," *Symposium*, 3 (1932). [A valuable essay.]

Waggoner, Hyatt H. "Emily Dickinson: The Transcendent Self," *Criticism*, 7 (1965).

Warren, Austin, "Emily Dickinson," *Sewanee Review*, 65 (1957).

Winters, Yvor. "Emily Dickinson and the Limits of Judgment," *Maule's Curse*. Norfolk, Conn.: New Directions, 1938.

INDEX

Note: Fictional characters are entered in small capital letters. Emily Dickinson's poems are listed under her name by title and by their number listing in the Johnson edition of her poems.

Abraham, 36

Adam, 111

Amherst, Mass., 4, 7, 8, 9, 11, 14, 15, 17, 19, 24, 35, 43–45, 70, 76, 77, 79

Amherst Academy, 9, 13, 15

Amherst Cattle Show, 9, 19

Amherst College, 7, 9, 11, 13, 15, 19; commencement, 9

Anderson, Charles, 47, 59, 69, 72n, 90, 115, 120n

Arms, George, 69

Atlantic Monthly, 1, 4, 76

Bethlehem, 113

Bible, The, 8, 18, 35, 38, 48, 112, 113

Bingham, Millicent Todd, 11

Blake, William, 48

Bolts of Melody (Millicent Todd Bingham), 45

Boston, Mass., 2, 4, 7, 13

Bowdoin, Elbridge Gridley, 20

Bowles, Mary, 27, 29

Bowles, Samuel, 18, 23, 27–29, 30, 31, 32, 39, 40, 41, 42, 111

"Broad is the road that leads to death" (Isaac Watts), 8

Brontë, Emily, 43

Brontë sisters, 76

Browning, Elizabeth Barrett and Robert, 76

Bryant, William Cullen, 57

Calvary, California, 25, 92

Calvin, John, 108

Calvinism, 7–8, 35, 37, 94, 96, 108, 109, 122, 123

Cambridge, Mass., 7

Capsule of the Mind, The (Theodora Ward), 22

Chase, Richard, 20, 38

Child, Lydia Maria, 18

Christ, 8, 24, 36, 74, 77, 81, 92–93, 98, 100, 115

Christianity, 14, 80, 81

Christian Psalmody (Isaac Watts), 51

Civil War, 36, 76, 78
Clark, Charles H. and James D., 26
Congregationalism, 8
Connecticut River Valley, 7
Cornell College, Iowa, 65n
Cummings, E. E., 49

David, King, 113
"Deacon's Masterpiece, The" (Oliver Wendell Holmes), 109
"Death of an Infant, The" (Lydia H. Sigourney), 32–33
"Decoration" (Thomas Wentworth), 109
Dickens, Charles, 27, 76
Dickinson, Austin (brother), 10, 11, 12, 13, 20, 21, 22, 27, 28, 40, 42, 79
Dickinson, Edward (father), 3, 5, 9–10, 11, 12, 13, 18, 20, 21, 24, 29, 39, 79, 109, 111
Dickinson, Elizabeth (aunt), 13
Dickinson, Emily: biography, 7–45; birth (1830), 7
  childhood, 12–14
  comparison with: the Bible, 70, 72; Bryant, 57; Cummings, 49; Edwards, 38, 80, 94; Emerson, 46, 57; Frost, 70, 117, 123; Hawthorne, 40, 95, 124; Higginson, 109; Holmes, 109; James, 95; Lanier, 51; Melville, 64; Poe, 46, 54, 93, 122; Robinson, 79; Sigourney, 32–33; Taylor, 90; Thoreau, 31, 36, 37; Twain, 102; Whitman,
  51, 93, 122; Whittier, 59; Wordsworth, 114
  conversation, 5, 17
  criticism by: Anderson, 47–48, 59, 69, 72n, 90, 115; Arms, 69; Bowles, 32; Chase, 20, 38; Gelpi, 38n; Griffith, 80n, 82n; Higginson, 3; Holland, 21, 32; Jackson, 41; Johnson, 94–95, 112; Manley, 100; Marcus, 56, 70; Monteiro, 105; Sewall, 25n; Stamm, 50n; Tate, 8; Toft, 65n; Ward, 14, 22, 23; Whicher, 9, 19, 25; Wilbur, 37; Winters, 74
  criticism of: Whitman, 3
  death (1886), 43
  definitive edition of her poetry, 20, 45
  description of, 4–5, 12, 17, 39, 40, 43
  desire for fame, 31, 72n, 122
  early poetry, 19, 20
  education, 13–15, 16
  first poem published—"Awake ye muses nine" (1850), 19
  legends about, 5, 20
  love crisis, 4, 5, 18, 22–29
  love for Judge Otis Lord, 41–42
  mannerisms, 5, 39
  "Master Letters," 22, 23, 24–25, 27, 28
  manuscripts, 43
  New England background, 7–9, 30
  personality, 2–5, 10–11, 20–21

philosophy, 18–19, 30, 34–35, 36, 37–38, 122–123

physical breakdown, 23–24, 25, 25n, 43

poetic theory, 46–48

prose, 13, 14, 21, 40, 79

posthumous fame, 34, 45, 123

publication, 3, 4, 12, 19–20, 31–32, 43–45

reading, 16, 18, 20, 25n, 76

reasons for writing, 22–24, 31

religion, 8, 14, 16, 21, 34–36, 38, 111–112, 122–123

seclusion, 5, 21, 24, 25, 28–29, 39–40, 122

stylistic traits, 2, 3, 13–14, 17, 47–52, 90, 123

themes: circumference, 3, 35, 38, 46, 58, 112, 113, 125; death, 8, 12–13, 33–34, 52–55, 101–110, 124; immortality, 8, 36, 111–121, 124; love, 22–29 *passim*, 81–93, 124; marriage, 22, 23, 28, 87, 89–93, 124; nature, 56–75, 123–124; pain, 8, 23, 94–101, 124; social scene, 76–81

works:

"A Bee his burnished Carriage," (1339), 60, 87

"A Bird came down the Walk," (328), 61–62 (quoted)

"A Clock stopped," (287), 107–109 (quoted)

"A Field of Stubble, lying sere," (1407), 78

"A Light exists in Spring," (812), 66–67 (quoted), 123

"A narrow Fellow in the Grass," (986), 32, 63–64 (quoted)

"A Route of Evanescence," (1463), 60 (quoted), 123

"A solemn thing—it was—I said," (271), 91n

"A Solemn thing within the Soul," (483), 116–117

"A Thought went up my mind today," (701), 95

"A Wife—at Daybreak I shall be," (461), 91n

"Abraham to kill him," (1317), 35–36

"After great pain, a formal feeling comes," (341), 23, 99–101 (quoted), 124

"Again—his voice is at the door," (663), 88

"All Circumstances are the Frame," (820), 56

"Although I put away his life," (366), 88n

"An altered look about the hills," (140), 66

"Apparently with no surprise," (1624), 57

"As by the dead we love to sit," (88), 30

"As imperceptibly as Grief," (1540), 14, 67–68 (quoted)

"Because I could not stop for Death," (712), 52–55 (quoted), 102, 124

"Because that you are going," (1260), 89n

Emily Dickinson—works (cont.)

"Bees are Black, with Gilt Surcingles," (1405), 59–60 (quoted)

"Behind Me—dips Eternity," (721),114–116(quoted),124

"Blazing in Gold and quenching in Purple," (228), 58 (quoted)

"Come slowly—Eden," (211), 22, 87

"Dare you see a Soul *at the White Heat,*" (365), 87

"Dust is the only Secret," (153), 102

"Essential Oils—are wrung," (675), 47

"Experience is the Angled Road," (910), 95

"Further in Summer than the Birds," (1068), 65n, 73–75 (quoted), 123–124

"Given in Marriage unto Thee," (817), 93

"Great Streets of silence led away," (1159), 117–118 (quoted)

"He fumbles at your Soul," (315), 24, 79–80

"He preached upon 'Breadth' till it argued him narrow," (1207), 79

"Heaven is so far of the Mind," (370), 52 (quoted)

" 'Heavenly Father'—take to thee," (1461), 36

"How happy is the little Stone," (1510), 72–73

"How many times these low feet staggered," (187), 105–106

"I cannot live with You," (640), 22, 88n

"I dreaded that first Robin, so," (348), 57, 98

"I felt a Funeral, in my Brain," (280), 23, 104–105 (quoted)

"I got so I could take his name," (293), 22, 88–89 (quoted)

"I have a Bird in spring," (5), 20

"I heard a Fly buzz—when I died," (465), 102–104 (quoted), 106, 124

"I know some lonely Houses off the Road," (289), 77

"I like to see it lap the Miles," (585), 76–77 (quoted)

"I live with Him—I see His face," (463), 88n

"I measure every Grief I meet," (561), 95–96 (quoted)

"I never felt at Home—Below," (413), 112

"I rose—because He sank," (616), 22

"I should have been too glad, I see," (313), 89–90

"I started Early—Took my Dog," (520), 82n, 82–84 (quoted), 84

"I taste a liquor never brewed," (214), 31–32, 113

"I tie my Hat—I crease my Shawl," (443), 49

"If you were coming in the Fall," (511), 87

"I'll tell you how the Sun rose," (318), 57

"I'm ceded—I've stopped being Theirs," (508), 87

"I'm 'wife'—I've finished that," (199), 91n

"In Winter in my Room," (1670), 82n, 84–85 (quoted)

"It sifts from Leaden Sieves," (311), 69

"It sounded as if the Streets were running," (1397), 59

"It was not Death, for I stood up," (510), 96–97 (quoted)

"It will be Summer—eventually," (342), 67

"I've seen a Dying Eye," (547), 105

"Lay this Laurel on the One," (1393), 109–110 (quoted)

"Like Brooms of Steel," (1252), 69

"Mine—by the Right of White Election," (528), 23, 91–92 (quoted), 124

"More Life—went out—when He went," (422), 109

"My Cocoon tightens—Colors tease," (1099), 117

"My life closed twice before its close," (1732), 25–26

"My Life had stood—a Loaded Gun," (754), 85–86 (quoted), 124

"New feet within my garden go," (99), 66

"No Brigadier throughout the Year," (1561), 60

"No Crowd that has occurred," (515), 113 (quoted)

"Of all the Souls that stand create," (664), 91

"Of Bronze—and Blaze," (290), 70–72 (quoted), 123

"Of God we ask one favor," (1601), 36

"One of the ones that Midas touched," (1466), 60

"Pink—small—and punctual," (1332), 59 (quoted)

"Publication—is the Auction," (709), 32

"Renunciation—is a piercing Virtue," (745), 98–99 (quoted), 124

"Safe in their Alabaster Chambers," (216), 2 (quoted), 44 (facsimile), 119–121 (quoted), 124

"She lay as if at play," (369), 32–34 (quoted), 102

"She rose to His Requirement —dropt," (732), 91n

"She sweeps with many-colored Brooms," (219), 57

"So give me back to Death," (1632), 110

"Some keep the Sabbath going to Church," (324), 31, 112

Emily Dickinson—works (cont.)

"Some—Work for Immortality," (406), 50–51 (quoted)

"Somewhere upon the general Earth," (1231), 89n

"Success," (67), 31, 37 (quoted), 41, 95

"Tell all the Truth but tell it slant," (1129), 46

"That after Horror—that 'twas us," (286), 97–98 (quoted)

"The Bat is dun, with wrinkled Wings," (1575), 64–65 (quoted)

"The Bible is an antique Volume," (1545), 112–113 (quoted)

"The Brain—is wider than the Sky," (632), 95

"The Brain, within it's Groove," (556), 95

"The farthest Thunder that I heard," (1581), 113–114 (quoted)

"The first Day's Night had come," (410), 97

"The Gentian weaves her fringes," (18), 67

"The last Night that She lived," (1100), 106

"The Morning after Wo," (364), 57

"The most pathetic thing I do," (1290), 89n

"The Mushroom is the Elf of Plants," (1298), 62–63 (quoted)

"The only Ghost I ever saw," (274), 77

"The Only News I know," (827), 111 (quoted)

"The Poets light but Lamps," (883), 124–125 (quoted)

"The Popular Heart is a Cannon first," (1226), 77

"The Rat is the concisest Tenant," (1356), 63 (quoted)

"The Snake" (see "A narrow Fellow in the Grass")

"The Soul selects her own Society," (303), 38, 81–82 (quoted)

"The Soul's Superior instants," (306), 113

"The Way I read a Letter's— this," (636), 88n

"The Wind begun to knead the Grass," (824), 58 (quoted)

"There came a Day at Summer's full," (322), 22, 88

"There came a Wind like a Bugle," (1593), 58–59 (quoted)

"There's a certain Slant of light," (258), 69–70

"There's been a Death, in the Opposite House," (389), 49 (quoted), 78–79 (quoted)

"These are the days when Birds come back," (130), 68–69 (quoted), 123

"They say that 'Time assuages,' " (686), 23

"This Consciousness that is

aware," (822), 94 (quoted)

✓"This is my letter to the World," (441), 31 (quoted)

"This World is not Conclusion," (501), 116 (quoted)

"Those not live yet," (1454), 118–119 (quoted), 124

"Though the great Waters sleep," (1599), 117

"Through the strait pass of suffering," (792), 28

"Till Death—is narrow Loving," (907), 81

" 'Tis so much joy! 'Tis so much joy," (172), 87

"Title divine—is mine," (1072), 23, 28, 92–93 (quoted), 124

"Too cold is this," (1135), 106–107 (quoted)

" 'Twas a long Parting—but the time," (625), 91n

" 'Twas like a Maelstrom, with a notch," (414), 96

"Two Lengths has every Day," (1295), 117 (quoted)

"Victory comes late," (690), 28

"What mystery pervades a well," (1400), 56

"What Soft—Cherubic Creatures," (401), 49 (quoted), 80–81 (quoted)

"Who occupies this House," (892), 78

✓"Wild Nights—Wild Nights," (249), 22

"You constituted Time," (765), 89n

"You said that I 'was Great' —one Day," (738), 88–89n

"Your Riches—taught me— Poverty," (299), 19

"You've seen Balloons set— Haven't You," (700), 77–78

Dickinson, Emily Norcross (mother), 3, 11, 39, 42

Dickinson family, 9, 11, 27, 31, 42, 79

Dickinson, Gilbert (nephew), 42–43, 109

Dickinson, Lavinia (sister— "Vinnie"), 12, 13, 26, 39, 43–45

Dickinson, Samuel Fowler (grandfather), 9

Dickinson, Susan Gilbert (Austin's wife), 11, 20, 21, 27, 31, 42, 43

Eden, 22, 87, 111, 113

Edwards, Jonathan, 7, 35, 38, 80, 94

Egyptians, 92

Eliot, George, 76

Emerson, Ralph Waldo, 4, 8, 18–19, 37, 46, 48, 57

"Emily Dickinson: Poetry and Punctuation," (Edith Stamm), 50n

Emily Dickinson's Poetry: Stairway of Surprise (Charles R. Anderson), 47

mily Dickinson: The Mind of the Poet (Albert J. Gelpi), 38n

nmons, Henry Vaughan, 20, 27

say on Man, An (Alexander Pope), 16

zekiel, 107

ulkner, William, 5

"ire and Ice," (Robert Frost), 117

rost, Robert, 70, 117, 123

abriel, 36

elpi, Albert J., 38n

enesis, 115

eneva, Switzerland, 107

enteel Tradition, 2, 59

ilbert, Susan (see Susan Gilbert Dickinson)

od, 7, 8, 10, 21, 23, 26, 35, 36, 38, 57, 65, 66, 67, 70, 71, 72, 81, 82, 88, 89–90, 91, 92, 98, 99, 102, 103, 106, 108, 111–112, 114, 115, 117, 122

oldsmith, Oliver, 16

ould, John, 18, 19

RANGERFORD, EMMELINE (Huckleberry Finn), 102

raves, John, 27

RIERSON, EMILY (*A Rose for Emily*), 5

riffith, Clark, 80n, 82n

rimshaw, William, 16

ampshire, 7, 10

arte, Bret, 32

Harvard College, 10, 11, 13

Hawthorne, Nathaniel, 40, 95, 124

"The heavens declare the glory of God; and the firmament sheweth his handywork," (Psalm 19), 70

Higginson, Thomas Wentworth, 1–5 passim, 10, 12, 13, 18, 22, 25, 25n, 26, 28, 30, 31, 32, 39, 40, 41, 43, 45, 48, 86, 93, 109, 111, 122

Holland, Dr. Josiah, 21, 31, 32, 41, 42, 76

Holland, Mrs. Elizabeth, 21, 30, 36

Holland family, 21, 26

Holmes, Oliver Wendell, 109

Huckleberry Finn (Mark Twain), 102

Humphrey, Jane, 14

Humphrey, Leonard, 15

Hunt, Edward B., 18

Jackson, Helen Hunt, 32, 40–41

Jacob, 36

James, Henry, 95

Johnson, Thomas H., 20, 45, 94–95, 112

Judas, 113

Lanier, Sidney, 51

Leaves of Grass (Walt Whitman), 3, 4, 32

"Letter to a Young Contributor"

(Thomas Wentworth Higginson), 1, 2
Letters from New York (Lydia Maria Child), 18
Lincoln, Abraham, 36
Lind, Jenny, 19
Long Shadow: Emily Dickinson's Tragic Poetry, The (Clark Griffith), 80n
Longfellow, Henry Wadsworth, 2, 32
Lord, Judge Otis, 26, 40, 41–43, 111, 121
Luke, 72
Lyman Letters, The (Richard B. Sewall), 25n
Lyon, Mary, 15, 16

Manley, Frank, 100
MARCHIONESS (*The Old Curiosity Shop*), 27
Marcus, Mordecai, 56, 70
Marvel, Ik (Donald Grant Mitchell), 20
Masque of Poets, A, 41
Melville, Herman, 64
"Merlin," (Ralph Waldo Emerson), 46
Midas, 60
Miller, Joaquin, 32
Miriam, 92
Moby Dick (Herman Melville), 4
Monteiro, George, 105
Moses, 36
Mount Holyoke Seminary, 13, 15, 19

"Narrative of Surprising Conversions" (Jonathan Edwards), 80
"New England Culture and Emily Dickinson" (Allen Tate), 8
New Testament, 77
Newton, Benjamin F., 18, 19, 21, 26, 42, 111
Norcross cousins, 30, 39, 40
Norcross, Frances, 30
Norcross, Louise, 30
Northampton, Mass., 7, 13, 19, 24, 27
"Notes on the Mind" (Jonathan Edwards), 94

"Ode: Intimations of Immortality from Recollections of Early Childhood" (William Wordsworth), 114
Old Curiosity Shop, The (Charles Dickens), 27
Old Testament, 106–107
Orpheus, 113

"Personal Narrative" (Jonathan Edwards), 38
Philadelphia, Pa., 24
Poe, Edgar Allan, 32, 46, 54, 93, 122
Poems of Emily Dickinson, The, edited by Thomas H. Johnson, 20
Pope, Alexander, 16
"Psalm of Life, A" (Henry Wadsworth Longfellow), 2

Puritanism, 122
Puritans, 36

Religious Revivals, 7, 8, 16
Revelation, 92, 120
Reveries of a Bachelor (Ik Marvel), 20
"Rhodora, The" (Ralph Waldo Emerson), 57
Robinson, Edwin Arlington, 79
Root, Abiah, 14, 15
"Rose for Emily, A" (William Faulkner), 5

Satan, 113
Scribner's Monthly, 21, 76
Sewall, Richard B., 25n
Shakespeare, William, 15, 48, 60
Sigourney, Mrs. Lydia, 32, 34
"Sinners in the Hands of an Angry God" (Jonathan Edwards), 16
South Hadley, Mass., 15
Spencer, Mr., 77
Springfield, Mass., 21
Springfield Republican, 21, 27, 31, 76, 77
Stamm, Edith, 50n
Stoddard, Solomon, 7
SWIVELLER, DICK (*The Old Curiosity Shop*), 27

Tate, Allen, 8
Taylor, Edward, 90
Tempest, The (William Shakespeare), 60

"That awful day will surely come" (Isaac Watts), 8
This Was a Poet (George Whicher), 9
Thoreau, Henry David, 31, 36, 37
Tillich, Paul, 37
"To a Waterfowl" (William Cullen Bryant), 57
Todd, Mabel Loomis, 12, 43–45
Toft, Robert J., 65n
TOM SAWYER, 77
"Trailing Arbutus, The" (John Greenleaf Whittier), 59
Transcendentalism, 8, 18–19, 35, 37, 56, 96, 122

Unitarianism, 8

Wadsworth, Rev. Charles, 18, 21, 24–29 *passim,* 40, 42, 92, 111
Ward, Theodora, 14, 22, 23
Washington, D.C., 24
Washington, George, 36
Watts, Isaac, 51
Western Reserve College, 9
Whicher, George, 9, 19, 25
Whitman, Walt, 2, 3, 4, 32, 51, 65, 93, 122
Whitney, Maria, 29, 40
Whittier, John Greenleaf, 59
Wilbur, Richard, 37
Willis, Nathaniel Parker, 32
Winstead, Ct., 77
Wintors, Yvor, 74
Worcester, Mass., 1, 18, 19
Wordsworth, William, 114